Golden-Brown Indian Girl

A Small Voice Gets **LOUDER**

Donna F. Council

ISBNs: 979-8-9856390-0-1 (softcover); 979-8-9856390-1-8 (ebook)

Library of Congress Control Number: 2022902754

Cover and interior by Mayfly Design

"People who lose everything that they have. . . the most important thing to them is their dignity. The extent to which we don't allow them to speak to the rebuilding process erodes the dignity that they have . . . and therefore, they need to be at the table at every phase of the recovery efforts."

—Russell Jones, PhD, psychologist and trauma specialist

Contents

Preface

Golden-Brown Indian Girl: A Small Voice Gets LOUDER is the true story of what happened to me, four of my sisters, and many other Native American children who were taken from our parents and put in boarding schools sanctioned by the US Government's Bureau of Indian Affairs and run by the Catholic Church. The irreparable damage to my family was done in the 1960s, but the practice of dividing Indian families had been going on in the US since the early 1800s.

My story is also about the long-lasting effects of severe child abuse on a human being who spent many years pushing the traumatic memories into my unconscious. And when I was finally ready to do the research to find out why this happened to me, and to so many others, I was horrified to find that all associated records concerning these events did not even exist.

I do not share every detail and every memory; but I hope that sharing many of my experiences will help other Native elders come forward and tell their truths, so that their healing can begin.

Chapter 1

The News

On an overcast day in May 2013, I was multitasking, cleaning house and doing laundry. I turned on the TV and sat down to fold towels. I turned the channel to the evening news and fell into shock. The local Twin Cities newscaster announced that the Catholic Church was being sued for sexually abusing children who were now adults.

I sat still, feeling anxious, wanting to cry yet again.

To be honest, I didn't want to feel those painful feelings anymore. But the news brought back terrible memories of Marty, the St. Paul's Indian Mission Boarding School that I was forced to attend on the edge of the Yankton Reservation in, Marty, South Dakota—and how my home life was disrupted when I was a young girl taken from my parents and my beloved Dakota/Lakota *tiospaye* (tribal clan) community.

I fell into that dark hole once again. I felt terrified; I had to talk to someone.

Later that evening, my husband and I watched the world news together. I told him about the attorneys who were taking the Catholic Church to court for sexually abusing children. He noticed that I was quiet and asked what I was thinking. I was remembering all the cruelty as though it were yesterday. It never really left me. I too had been abused as a child at the hands of the Catholic Church.

All these years later, I felt so thankful for the two gentlemen, Jeff Anderson and Patrick J. Wall, the attorneys who had the courage to take on the Catholic Church's sex abuse scandal. They worked hard to get the Minnesota Child Victims Act passed, which lifted the statute of limitations on reporting childhood sex abuse.

The law was a long time coming. After generations of efforts by the so-called "sacred" Holy Catholic Church to cover them up, their sins of abuse of young White children finally caught peoples' attention. But Indian children had known this long history from one generation to the next. I was the second generation of my family who was made to go to an Indian boarding school and to never, *ever* talk about it. I can only imagine how many on my father's side of the family had experienced the same physical and psychological cruelty and abuse, yet a little bit harsher, more brutal, some even dying.

Ignoring the emotional signals and reminders of the trauma over many years had a way of stopping time for me; I had disregarded them and pushed them aside to somewhere deep into my subconscious. For that reason I remembered much of it only in bits and pieces. I had wanted to just forget those times, skip those memories, because they only brought back ugly, distrustful, suspicious feelings. Painful feelings. Feelings about acts of abuse that I had never fully revealed to anyone.

At the same time, I was elated. *Wow! This is on TV, letting the world know that the Catholic Church was not who they pretended to be: holy, helping the poor.*

I wanted to hear that this news was for *all* children who had been abused by the Catholic clergy—all the massive abuses that took place in horrible institutions just like where my little sisters and I were "housed." I have not considered or referred to them as schools, because a school is where young children should get a good education and have their growth and development nurtured—not experience emotional, physical, and sexual abuse, loss, abandonment, and separation from their parents.

I wanted the news to include a mention of all the Indian children who didn't have a voice, or a choice about being taken from their/our homes to be put in Indian boarding schools run by the Catholic Church, where they/we were abused. I wanted the news reports to contain more details of the Church's ugly history with Catholic Church Mission boarding schools and the Bureau of Indian Affairs (BIA) boarding schools, which were just as evil.

I decided I was going to call those Minnesota attorneys to share what happened to me and my little sisters at an early age, and describe where those traumatic events took place in South Dakota. But I held off calling them. I was too embarrassed, ashamed to tell anyone about my experience. It had been such a long time, more than fifty years.

~

Yes, it happened to me and my little sisters in the 1960s. And nothing was said openly among the Indian students who were forced to go through these horrific experiences. The Catholic Church told so many lies and hid the many secret crimes committed against children, for the protection of the reputations of guilty nuns and priests. I am only one of so many children who endured this treatment between 1816 and 1974. Abuse in many forms continued on without any punishment or a second thought for the Indian children because we were *"only Indians"* or *"those people."*

I can't speak or tell the abuse stories for other former Indian children. Many have died and taken their pain and unresolved grief to the grave. I can feel their emptiness, a deep sadness. I ask the creator, Waken Tankan, for peace for them and for us.

In some ways I never grew up, because I remained stuck in one of my nightmares about being at Marty all over again. All those sad thoughts built up and overwhelmed me. I didn't get a chance to deal with those feelings. I felt ashamed to say, "I'm a survivor." I'm alive, but I don't feel like I "survived" those boarding school days. I just existed and got by. After I left Marty, I've had a lifetime of struggle to shed the remnants from the abuse. You could say I survived, but the healing wasn't there.

I was so wrong to try so hard to block those memories; it hurts even more from not giving myself permission. I was too ashamed, like I was the one who was weak, bullied.

Over and over, again and again, that news story ripped open my heart, forcing me to relive the events that happened to me a long time ago. They say this happened so long ago, yet it felt as real as if it all happened just yesterday. Over all these years, I saw things that triggered memories of Marty—the smell of fresh cinnamon rolls, the smell of the soap that was used in the cafeteria to wash dishes and silverware—internalized scents that triggered sadness about what else happened so long ago.

~

My childhood traumas were part of a much larger generational trauma suffered by Native Americans in recent centuries, the US government's goal to "civilize" us. The laws were for the White Europeans, designed only for their gain of Indian land. Native peoples had difficulty understanding all the rules and laws in a second language (English). Indians' only choice was to assimilate as best they/we could. History books still don't tell the whole truth about how Indian people were treated as less than human, and how reservations and mission Indian boarding schools were forced on Native people, causing the breakdown and destruction of native families and communities. The original 1924 version of the Indian Citizenship Act included swearing not to live the Indian life, and we still couldn't vote or learn the true high cost our ancestors were forced to pay.

In the past (prior to our "assimilation"), an Indian person was self-identified by their tribe. One's tribe language was an essential and strong part of Indian identity. But Indians growing up in my parents' generation, from teens to the elderly, were told not to speak their own language, or they would be punished. If an Indian person spoke their Native language, the entire Indian community was punished, either by not getting any food ration or by sending away the children to learn how *not* to be Indian. Even though government or mission Indian boarding schools are no longer operated by the Bureau of Indian Affairs or the Catholic Church, the long-term damage persists. Reservation life is the poorest in the nation, with no way out, no jobs, the breakup of families, and the absence of kinship with the community.

Indian people are tribal people, each tribe supported their own form of government. Each individual was important. All were respected, and all had a role in the community. But we no longer have the tribal council's circle or society. Our ways have changed, and from generation to generation we see the evidence of how essential community is to our survival as a people. Knowing what role I have, teaching and receiving guidance from the community, the sense of belonging nurtures the soul, mind, and body. These elements are vital. Each lesson continues the circle, and the community grows stronger because of the people and the community. However, people suffering indignity in the community impacts everything. The family's beliefs evaporate; individuals question who they are. They ask, "Where are the people who are just like me?"

We need to connect, be part of a community.

~

It happened finally. In one moment, I got courage. I finally got the nerves to do it, but I was scared even as I made the call to the Minnesota attorneys.

The little voice said, *Don't you dare say a thing. Don't mention . . . don't say how . . .*

I wrestled with that little voice of the little golden-brown Indian girl.

I listened to the rings. *Hang up!*

Another part of me thought, *One more ring, just to say you called.*

An answering machine came on. *What a relief, good.*

I left a message, thinking, *They won't call me back.*

Yet the same tiny little voice said, *Call back.*

I told myself, *Let go. No way would I want to bring up the pain of these days, of being placed at that boarding school. Painful.*

I myself, and many other Indian elders, knew and experienced the true experiences of being forced to leave our families and live in the Catholic Church mission boarding schools. I don't know if any of us have made peace with what it took from us at a very young age. No one has been held accountable for the abuse we suffered as children that made it so hard for us to speak up, having no faith or belief that our voices would be heard. Even now, I can't help feeling it will fall on deaf ears just like before. But I need to state my opinion clearly: the Catholic Church was not innocent of child abuse, sexual abuse, physical abuse, verbal abuse, or the religious indoctrination abuse style that was forced on Indian children for so long.

I'm only one of many voices, but our message needs to be heard. This story tells the truth of what happened to me and my four little sisters in the sixties. I'm older now, no longer that meek little brown girl who was the product of a Catholic mission boarding school.

~

My phone rang.

"This is Patrick J. Wall." The attorney was calling back to follow up.

Oh no. My stomach dropped. I felt like the child once again.

I started crying, sharing my stories about Marty with him, telling him that the same abuse happened to me and many other Indian children. "What happened to me and my sisters was just as bad and worse than what happened to the clients you are representing."

He was very understanding. He knew about Marty and the abuse of children placed there from the Yankton Sioux tribe. the Dakota tribe.

He said, "I believe you; your pain is real."

I appreciated that he knew about it and acknowledged my pain. I felt encouraged to start addressing the emotional anguish I had held in for so many years. I begin to think of healing instead of stuffing my feelings even deeper.

He went on to tell me how South Dakota threw the allegations out of court, saying that the abuses of Indian children in Catholic Church-run schools happened too long ago—beyond the statute of limitations. No cases had been filed on behalf of Indian children against the Catholic Indian Mission school in South Dakota in that small window of time. He explained that his case was only in Minnesota law, that the South Dakota legislature "refuses even to hear it."

The Indians were left out again. Erased. Still silenced.

I was appalled. I became angry, learning that the South Dakota legislature will never have the Church admit to, or be held accountable for, a long history of child abuse in the Indian boarding schools. *Shame on you, South Dakota!*

Their statute of limitations law says to me, "Get over it, because it happened so long ago."

The message I heard clearly was that I don't deserve to have the right to address my offenders: the nuns, the priests, or the Church. Hearing of that injustice felt like being abused all over again. How can you put a time limit on emotional trauma that lingers for many years? No one just "gets over" horrible childhood trauma quickly or easily—not the trauma that is hidden, never talked about, minimized. The trauma that no matter how much it bothers you later in life, that, even when asked, you volunteer "only enough" information about your past years in a boarding school to prevent further discussion.

I was upset in retrospect that I was only one small voice that wasn't loud enough or confident enough to say, "Look what happened to me and all the other Indian children who suffered from the Church and Bureau of Indian Affairs schools."

My little sisters and I did not volunteer to attend that school. We had no choice. I was a minor and a Native American Indian child who was a part of the US government's effort to take me away from my family and assimilate me and my little sisters into mainstream White society by destroying our Native culture, language, history, self-esteem, and dignity. But now for the first time, I could hear the little voice loud and clear. The golden-brown Indian girl was no longer whispering, no longer a meek little voice afraid to speak: *I have the right to have the court know that I was abused physically and emotionally as a child, and that it caused trauma that continues through my adulthood!*

Who's going to answer for all the Church abusers' wrongdoing that destroyed so many young lives? The school didn't have my best interests or even my actual education in mind. I was forced to learn everything about Catholic beliefs and suffer "corrective" physical punishment if I went against "the Church."

To overlook extreme inequities on so many levels was a serious mistake by the government Bureau of Indian Affairs (BIA). No means of justice was available for us. Indian children had to struggle and suffer emotional anguish all those years—and no one thought to ask, "At what price?—What after-effects would these children experience in their adult lives from their childhood traumas?"

Back in those days, Indians didn't have access to counseling of any kind; therapy was unheard of in those times. Staying in denial was easier when there was no other recourse. Enormous effort was needed to try to appear normal; I had to swallow the lump in my throat of hurt again and again. And feeling all alone, I figured it must be *me* that is the problem. What else could it be? I was unable to close that chapter of my life.

All the shame and guilt from the trauma wounds created a form of PTSD (post-traumatic stress syndrome). Indian children placed in these institutions of learning were emotionally injured, and not from going into battle in a war in some foreign land—it happened right here in the United States. No guns were used by the nuns, priests, or the Church—just forceful attempts to convert you against your will with lies, misleading information, and more abuse.

~

Ours is a history of genocide. To try to figure out what went wrong, one has to know the real history about what happened to Indian children and whole tribes of people.

When the White establishment tried to exterminate the Indians, and terminate our culture and traditions, no questions were asked. It was just that way. Indians did not have the rights or privileges that others (Whites mostly) could take for granted. The US government broke all their treaties with my people.

To this day I see Indian people having less, not having opportunities to better ourselves due to conditions left over from past treatment of Indian Nations, the continuing disparity from being violated and ignored.

Indian people were never oppressed by choice; and we never wanted a handout. We would be happy just to have back the resources we had always used to survive, including our language and our culture. We are a tribal people; we need each other in order to pass our ways on to the next generation. If we don't continue to be proud and willing to encourage and empower the younger generation, we will no longer exist. We will be assimilated, erased.

That was the point really.

We were being erased.

Maybe I could believe that correcting one wrong has some value, even if it won't benefit or heal any previously harmed Indian children. But at least the truth is now out there. No more hiding the Church's shameful past. The truth is exposed to all who thought the Catholic Church was gracious and holy. The truth has to be heard and accepted. The bad memories and the painful history carried out at the hands of the Catholic Church in mission schools on the reservations have certainly not been forgotten by those who were abused—the Indian children who suffered abuse for years. Hopefully they/we will find some healing now as adults.

The 1819 United States Congress provided funds for education to "civilize" Indians. The Christian schools were started and first run by White Christian missionaries with a goal to assimilate Indians into White culture, but without any of the same White privileges. Institutional racism was widely embedded in all laws related to "regulating" the Indian nations.

Churches, schools, and social opinion falsely accused us of being pagans who didn't believe in God. They denied that Indian people were spiritual people who believed in the Creator of all. We didn't call our Creator by the same name they did.

To know and feel that our own race is so hated is a painful experience. To be placed in educational institutions bent on destroying, killing all aspects of our culture, the genocide that was evident on all levels, was inexplicable to our people. Children were harmed and beaten so badly, they died from injuries. Early Indian people did not comprehend the White man's rationale or greed over a piece of land and a mineral, gold.

If the walls of the White-run boarding schools could talk, they would tell the stories of the children who suffered at the hand of the righteous, God-fearing White people, and how children were touched by pedophiles who prayed every day for forgiveness.

Rapes were never talked about, nor were the perpetrators revealed by the young ones who killed themselves, feeling ashamed, blaming themselves for assaults they had no control over. Those crimes committed against Indian children, and some adults, were met with no justice.

Indians had no rights—legal, social, ethical—we had no right to be anything. From the very beginning, Indians were looked at differently—we didn't measure up to White society. We were different, seen as a threat. Even becoming citizens in 1924 didn't guarantee being treated well or experiencing respect. We could join the military and fight to protect America; yet we weren't good enough to have the legal rights to protect our culture, language, religion, or choose how we will be educated.

The hidden psychological and emotional abuse the Catholic Church did to damage White children carried into their entire lives too. And they need to tell their stories. But justice is unbalanced for Indian children, because the laws about what happened so long ago have only protected those individuals who don't look like us. We never had the chance to be heard or respected in regard to childhood traumas that have never healed.

I was that child who heard again and again, "You're just an Indian." Abuse was my history with a Catholic Church that taught me that God's message was: I don't matter. I and so many others were taught to mask our feelings.

The Church clergy took away my security in an institution, in a religious setting. How is it possible for any child to understand the messages in the words of God when preached by the same predators who perverted the meanings by preying upon and victimizing that child?

When authority figures treat you so badly, and you have no choice but to follow their every rule in a tightly controlled environment, the result is psychological and emotional harm. Having no freedoms or recourse caused extreme anxiety and took away our voices. The nuns, priests, and brothers who committed crimes against children in many Indian boarding schools committed unspeakable harm, causing lifelong psychological damage. Harsh corporal punishment and emotional abuse cause damage to any child's overall mental health and sense of well-being.

We were left to cry in silence and never to talk about it. No one listened or made an effort to find out how we were doing, and no one seemed to care. We didn't exist at all in that horrible place. Once when my little sister saw me cry, she tried to comfort me and tell me I would be okay. I felt so bad that she saw me cry, because I should have been there for my little sisters. We had no one to let us know they cared. Our mom couldn't write or call; she didn't have the education or opportunity to learn how to write. Our family didn't have a phone.

All I wanted to do was go home. I wish I could remember at least one good memory of my schooling. I feel my life is missing a complete sentence. Someone came along and erased it.

Trying to ignore the aftermath of whatever types of abuse we endured, helped us to avoid the inevitable blame and judgment by others. It was easy to make young children believe that whatever was done to us was well-deserved. We were at fault. After all, this was a "holy" Church where the "good people" were. The perpetrators manipulated children into believing that whatever was done to them (the "sinners") was done "for the love of God."

The Catholic Church went on condoning the abuse of children, just moving offenders to other places without punishment. Indian children were still bullied; nuns found others to torment. One seldom hears talk about the nuns' abuse of children; is that because they are women? Women are supposed to have that nurturing motherly quality; the nuns I have known are the total opposite. Taking their vows to "marry God" didn't mean they had insight into how to treat children.

I still don't understand why this abuse was allowed to continue for such a long time. Former students like myself are still in pain. I still feel ashamed to admit I was traumatized. I am not yet comfortable sharing much about it. I don't even feel I have the permission to be pissed off. I still know that visceral feeling of being despised at Marty.

Prayers have not restored my self-esteem or sense of dignity.

In my heart, I wish something could be done. If nothing else, I would like all the others who suffered to know it wasn't their fault, to begin talking about it openly, and to begin healing.

I saw that Pope Frances wrote an apology letter and statement regarding the former indigenous children being placed in residential Indian boarding schools. Not to disregard his apology, maybe it will bring some peace of mind to some. But a letter is a piece of paper, easy to disregard, file, or throw in the trash. A "sorry" just isn't acceptable to me or my sisters. The experience ruined my family. Can I get back all the emotional wellness of a childhood with healthy memories—not having to worry or stress out about wanting to play outside or laughing with my sisters, and perhaps the only concern being what might be for supper? No, a letter cannot take away the pain suffered at the hands of the Catholic Church. Straightforward, they were abusive while telling me their God is loving and forgiving and will keep me safe, and at the same time robbing each of us of our innocence. It was easy for them to go to mass and be forgiven, praying away their crime of hurting and violating helpless children.

If I were to be asked what I want in this situation, I know for sure it would not be monetary gifts or an apology. That would mean nothing.

I want my childhood back in some way, so my inner child could feel at ease—because her suffering has impacted everything about her. The damage and wounds are deep. The unfinished healing has caused great emotional anguish that still controls most of my life. Even a small event can cause me to fall into a deep sadness. I want to know some emotional calmness without fear of what is going to be said or done to me. Church clergy installed within me a "video player" full of ugly memories; I want them to shut off the recorder that continues to tell me that I'm the one to blame and that I got what I deserved.

Being terrorized as a child and being bullied caused stress in my life. The feelings come back in different forms—shapes, sounds, smells. If a person shouts loudly, I can go into fright "don't hurt me" mode. It comes racing back as I relive being bullied as a child.

I wished it to be publicly noted that it was not only White children who were sexually abused by the Catholic Church in the scandal that was covered on local and world news. I thought it might bring me some validation to put the Catholic Church on notice. I wanted the Catholic parishioners who go to Mass, who donate great money and follow faithfully, to know that Indian children and other children of color have also been abused by their Church. Someone needed to speak up on behalf of Indian children.

Chapter 2

My Tiospaye

I was six in 1960. I lived happily in Mitchell, South Dakota, with my parents and my six sisters (four younger and two older). I never knew what it was like to be hungry, let alone what it was like to be separated from our parents. My parents kept us together, making sure we were safe.

My parents did common labor, doing seasonal work for local farmers, picking potato and "shacking" green hay. Before combine machines for baling hay, farmers gathered hay by hand and stacked it into triangle shapes. My parents' combined income was less than a dollar a day. They got ready for work by filling jugs of water. My oldest sister took care of us until our parents come home. Our home was a large army tent, and our campsite was always near the fields where they were working. We didn't notice that we were poor. We always had what we needed; my father made sure of that.

I couldn't have been happier living in our tent. If we lived that way today, it would be like camping out; but for us then, the tent was home. Our father made a floor out of cardboard, so we wouldn't be sleeping on plain dirt. Cardboard also kept the floor from getting damp. Our living and sleep rooms were the inside of the tent. My parents were on one side, and my sisters and I were on the other side. My father made a place where we could have a cold wash, and kept water nearby. Our kitchen was an open pit my father made where my mother cooked and made bread, and made the morning coffee for my father. Smelling fresh coffee cooked outside was peaceful. I still remember the fresh morning dew air.

My father talked proudly about his Teton Oglala heritage. Being from the Pine Ridge Reservation, he was a "strong warrior" and a good provider who loved each one of us. Ihanktowan Yankton (meaning "people of the end village") was my mother's tribe. She was the one who actually kept our family going. We had three hot meals every day, and she always made extra food. If we were hungry, we could have something to eat. We had peanut butter, white flour, lard, dark and white syrup, corn meal, oatmeal, and a meat like spam. Not a big variety for cooking. If we had extra money, my mother bought bacon. We had potatoes, and she made homemade bread. We had a lot of soup. We had chickens, and sometimes deer meat.

Everything was provided for us kids. Our job was to play. The seven girls in our family were close in age. I always had someone to play with, talk to, and hang out with. We had some typical sibling rivalry, but we always got along. We had each other. I could not imagine being away from my sisters or my parents. Such an idea never even crossed my young mind. I never thought I wanted anything more. I never wished for anywhere fancier to live. We were happy.

In the winter months, we went back to a small house in Ravinia, and my two older sisters went to school. Our house had no heat or running water and no inside bathroom. Having to haul our water, my father filled four to five cream cans for our weekly water use, for cooking and bathing. My mother did all the cooking on a wood-burning stove. No matter what happened, we were all together. We looked out for each other, we took care of each other. We played outside and had fun with our pets. We had nurturing, love, security, and a warm home.

~

As a child, I was taught that all people are human beings. Indian people know there is something greater than us humans and that life has a purpose, down to the smallest insects. I was told that we are a species that depends on and needs the earth in order to survive. We share the earth with all the other creatures who live on the land.

Lesson stories were a big part of growing up within my tiospaye. Our tiospaye included my extended family, uncles, aunties, cousins, and those not related who were adopted from another tribe; we all saw each other as relatives. Indian children learned by example, not by punishment. Elders took the time to show me how to do things more than once, until I knew how to do whatever the task was. Adults in my community shared their wisdom and guidance when children misbehaved. We were told "corrective" stories in a loving way.

Once when I was helping my mother cook supper, she told me a story about a time when she was a child. While helping her mother gather wild beans for dinner, my mother found and took some wild beans from a badger hole. Like all creatures, the badger had gathered and stored food for the coming winter months, and this badger had had a good harvest. My mother might have taken all the badger's beans without having any respect for the badger's hard work or the time the badger took to gather all these beans, but her mother had told her, "Only take what you need for the meal, and leave the rest for the badger. And be sure to very carefully put everything back the way you found it in and around the badger's hole."

One time when I went with my parents and my uncle and auntie to search for wild turnips, my uncle told me, "You have to be careful. You can't just be running in the fields without paying attention to what is around you. You could run into a rattlesnake."

He told me to also watch for poison ivy and itchy weed. "After all," he said, "we were entering spaces that belong to the plants and the rattlesnakes."

When we finally found some wild turnip plants, my uncle gently cleared some space around the plants. I was in a big hurry to pick and eat the turnips, but he took his time, showing me how to dig up the turnips properly without harming other plants. After we gathered a good harvest, he told me we could stop.

At that point, all I wanted to do was to eat the turnips. I loved the smell of fresh dirt, and I didn't mind eating turnips with dirt on them. I always had a craving for dirt. (I still do.)

My uncle smiled and explained simply, "If you eat up all the raw turnips, we will not have any to take home."

One time my father was fixing something in the shed. In a corner of the shed was a wasps' nest. I watched them go in and out. One climbed into a little hole and another flew out. I was curious to see what would happen if I knocked the nest down, so I picked up a rock and threw it at the nest. The wasps came out fast and flew around their nest. My father told me that I needed to stop, otherwise I could be stung. But I kept throwing rocks. I was stung in the corner of my eye. It swelled up really bad, and I couldn't see out of that eye.

My father said calmly, "You made wasps mad. That's why you got stung."

That day I learned another lesson: to listen more, be careful when you play with anything that might bite or sting.

Indian people often used great humor and stories in teaching lessons, big or small, to children. We had to listen closely, otherwise we might miss the opportunity to learn from the stories or experience the lesson from an elder or parent. We knew to "listen and learn."

I especially enjoyed when stories were told in our Dakota language the old way, which had a deeper meaning and was often very funny. My favorite ones were about *Iktomi*, a well-known spider-trickster in Lakota mythology. Hearing an Iktomi story was a privilege when all the chores were done. The stories made emotional connections, and I found it very exciting when one was told. This character, Iktomi, got himself into mischief, always trying to pull a fast one or trying to fool those around him. But his tricks usually blew up in his own face.

We knew to respect the Iktomi stories told by adults. They helped children look more closely at our own mischief, and see how Iktomi looked foolish in behaving the way he did. They taught us to have a sense of humor as part of a life lesson, and to have patience, to know that problems usually work out, and everything will eventually fall into place. We were taught that we should not rush to obtain earthly things out of greed or selfishness—or we will be fooled like Iktomi and end up with nothing, or just look plain foolish.

So I learned that if you are not aware of yourself or your surroundings, you can be fooled, or bitten by a rattlesnake. I learned to respect animals and to be careful not to hurt plants. I learned we cannot have everything in sight. We must take only what is needed to eat, and do not be wasteful. Never take what is not yours. I was taught to pray for personal guidance and to take care of Mother Earth. We honor her, we don't take more than what is needed.

I was taught to respect the thunderstorm; be quiet. I heard my mother asking the thunder and lightning not to do any harm; both are very powerful. The lighting from the thunder can cause fires; the wind can damage the biggest trees. Water is life, our body needs water, we pray with water and with cedar, sage, and sweet grass. We give thanks for the animals that feed us, not wasting food, we were free.

Hearing my relatives talk about growing up living "the Indian way" as "a good way"—laughing and joking with one another, taught me the value of living simply and having only what was needed to live and survive. I learned that being Indian is to be humble, not to brag about what we accomplish—or how much of this or that we have. To brag or show off about personal gains is "just not the Indian way." I learned it is an honor to be humble. Besides, the community already knows what all you have. Your actions or behaviors can be seen by others in the community.

We traveled back to the reservation to visit our tiospaye home, on my mother's side, to attend ceremonies and celebrations. On those occasions, the women all gathered together getting ready, cooking, happily talking and laughing while cutting meat for a soup. The soup had simple ingredients, meat and vegetables, no extra fancy spices added. The women made fry bread (flat dough bread). I helped. I liked to hang around my favorite auntie and listen to my mother and the other women relatives joking. They made it look easy to cook on an open fire.

The men started the fire and did the serving of the food. We would all eat, the kids would play, and my parents gathered with the other adults to hear the latest news.

The values taught us at home were to respect our elders, not to fight or do any kind of harm or bullying of another person. We were taught to care about how we would feel if we were hurt or bullied—our Golden Rule. I felt great respect for all my male relatives, my grandpa, uncles, cousins, and their teachings of great respect for my community of women—my mom, sisters, aunties, and nieces who gathered around the fire pit. It was fun to watch each one prepare food, make bread. I learned how important it is to listen to those voices deep inside you, telling you when something is wrong or too good to be true.

If we make a mistake, no judging, no shaming, we were encouraged to look at it another way. My community didn't punish us for getting anything wrong. We were encouraged to try again until it was done the way it was supposed to be done. The Indian way was to correct our mistakes, and learn from our mistakes. Parents allowed a child to learn a skill without any help from the adult.

If there was a difficult issue to address in our tiospaye, each adult had their own solution and shared lessons from their own wisdom. If a decision or choice made was an error, we were encouraged to look at the issue in another way, or gather what was needed for a ceremony (counseling) for more advice. If it wasn't the right time or place, the individual needing correction had to pay close attention and/or change their behavior or way of living.

A "true" Indian who values the good in people was naturally valued as trustworthy. Any leader had to first earn the trust of the people by consulting with others about important decisions. Good leaders earn the respect of the people to be able to talk on their behalf. My grandfather was such a wise elder. At a ceremony, he held an eagle feather in his hand and stroked it up and down. He kept it with him as he sang and prayed. After the ceremony, he greeted all the relatives. He told us that living our way is hard, yet he was happy.

He said, "The eagle feather teaches a powerful message."

He raised the feather, stroked it up and down, and held it up, saying, "This is our life. The Creator gave us each a life of one's own, to choose good or bad. Where we stand on this earth, we are only between worlds. Each feather stem, from top to bottom, is the Indian's life. If we rub the feather one way, it separates. But if we rub the feather the other way, it will return to its original shape. We have a choice about how we live. It's up to us."

~

My parents had suffered hardship, living in poverty. I used to listen to my relatives tell stories of the hard times. My mother was nine years old when she and her brother and sister lost their father. The family lost the only breadwinner—my grandfather, which caused hardship on the whole family. My grandmother became a widow and a single parent. They family traveled so her mother could find any kind of job in order to survive. They were homeless, and not having a home makes it harder to get a job. My mother's dream was to have a place to live without having to go to other people's houses to sleep for a night. The weather was harsh in the winters in South Dakota. Even with those losses, my mother was still able to learn gratitude. She lived without expectations for herself other than just surviving for that day. She said that material objects were not what was valuable.

Those older times were very difficult for displaced Indian families, and for all the Indian people. Indian Nations had lost most of the land they lived on and all their food sources from the land. They were isolated on a piece of reservation land with nothing but fields—an assigned area with restricted boundaries, like an invisible fence. With no local businesses and no proper shelters, the results were poverty, homelessness, hunger, and oppression. The reservation was a space without resources, limited to bare essentials necessary to survive. And leaving the reservation was a big risk, knowing Indians would be treated badly, even killed due to the extreme racism and hostility of the local farmers and the all-White townspeople.

My parents hoped my sisters and I would not have to experience the discrimination and hardships they had each experienced. My mother wanted her daughters to know how to deal with difficult encounters. Mom knew how dangerous it could be in her own childhood. When her family ventured out and ran into townspeople, they experienced verbal assaults, name-calling, and threats. Going back to the reservation was better for "staying safe and not ending up dead," according to my mother. Very seldom did any Indian person go to the local shopping area unless they had no choice. A White man would likely not even get into trouble for raping an Indian. Being unable to leave the reservation, Indians were not able to obtain any fresh or healthy food, only government rations that came once a month. The government rations weren't really much help to those who were without a permanent home—with nowhere to store commodities or to cook food. The unhealthy food, made up of starches, carbs, and fat, led to poor nutrition, poor health, and many diseases.

A friend once introduced me to her mother, and as we visited, she shared what she witnessed as a child living in a small town about an hour away from the reservation. Once a month, she saw Indian families come to town by wagon to pick up their government rations. Local townspeople sat on the other side of the road alongside the riverbank. They brought their chairs and sat on the riverbank to watch the Indians come. This was their entertainment.

The Indian wagons were full of large family groups, everyone from the very young to elders. The government-regulated ration controls made it hard for Indian people to get enough to feed all their family members. No other family member could pick up rations for anyone who was too young or too sick to come, or for elders who had trouble traveling on those days when the weather was too hot or very cold. Each individual parent, grandparent, and child had to show their own ration ticket.

My mother never forgot those days and what it was like to not have a bed, and to be hungry. Though she had a hard time, she was grateful and thankful for whatever she did have. Her dream was to always have a roof overhead. Material objects were not what was valuable to her. She wanted our family to look out for each other, love one another, and stay close to one another. I don't know how she dealt with all that pain pushed on Indians, or the oppressive reservation life that made sure Indians couldn't have a voice or the same privileges as the White man. I don't know how she dealt with emotional losses and traumas.

My mother had grown up in and was still a member of the Native American Church (NAC) and was a strong believer and a devoted NAC member. Due to the Catholic Church and missionaries of other faiths who had influence on the Indian community before my mother's time, NAC had begun to include teaching the Bible. NAC practiced the Cross-fire—a ceremonial prayer ritual at a fireplace, which usually included tobacco in our culture. But NAC didn't use tobacco, and they added biblical scriptures and other elements and symbols of Christianity.

I always went with my parents to the church meetings. My mother taught me how to make the ceremony bundles to be placed on a relative's grave, and how to fix the morning food. She did a lot of fundraising in the early days to give back to the Church community. Our parents decided to have all seven of us girls blessed in the Native American

Church, similar to being "baptized" in the White man's religion. However, I was taught that our Creator, Wakan Tanka, gave us gifts for us to survive, and we should never lose our Indian "ways." My mother told me I was loved and not judged for something I'm not. I was taught to respect the eagle feather, to honor the ways of the feathers, the drum. The music is so beautifully done in my native tongue. My grandpa, who ran the NAC service, always had good lessons to teach in the sermon—that my Creator was a good Creator.

Prior to 1978, *all* Indian ceremonies were forbidden. If Indians were caught in any, they could be prosecuted and sent to prison. If we wanted to pray, it had to be done in secrecy; it was risky. Not until the passage of the American Indian Religious Freedom Act (AIRFA) in 1978, were Native American Indians allowed to believe, express, and carry out our own traditional rites and ceremonies, use and possess sacred objects, and access our own religious sites.

The elder members passed on the teachings. Our church was never rich and had no large buildings, nothing fancy. It was very humble, like the members. They had tepee meetings. After the church meetings, my mom and aunties cooked on an open fire. When the food was ready, the men served all the church members. Those were happy times. We could hear Indian languages being spoken. The laughter was pleasing to my ears. Seeing my relatives laughing and smiling was what I knew about going to church. Our church was about "love."

My father grew up in Kyle, South Dakota. In his younger days, he rode bulls in the rodeos, and was very good working with horses. He took "first" many times. He couldn't do it professionally; the rodeos were run by Whites; he was Indian. Just like the times and people changed, so did the rodeo and part of my father. He made the major decision to move off the reservation when we were young. But we always traveled back to my mother's tribe, the Yankton Sioux, with "the people who live at end."

My father chose to stay close to my mother's side of our family. I often heard my father proudly say he is Teton Oglala, being from Pine Ridge, and he has a large tiospaye. He has three siblings who all had large families. One of my uncles had eight boys. We didn't get a chance to meet or get close to any of them.

His choice to not to live on his reservation was why we moved to the town of Mitchell. If we had stayed on the reservation, I don't know how we would have ended up. I understand why my father decided not to raise us on the reservation, he could see the bigger picture.

My father could do anything with his hands. He would work any place to take care of us and be a good husband and father. He sometimes left town to work and came home each weekend with a car full of food.

~

As we got older and started school, we fell victim to racial discrimination. Almost all the people who lived in Mitchell were White, and living in a White community for Indians meant being treated like dirt. My parents took the brunt of the discrimination then later we were treated the same. If we went into stores, we were treated rudely. Merchants ignored us and waited on others first no matter what. Many Indian people experienced trauma and pain from the way that people in White society treated us. We were told we should stay on the reservation (if we are not seen, then there was no problem); we are just drunks wearing feathers.

Being told "You're Indian" was something I didn't hear or feel until I started school, and the White teacher belittled me in front of the whole classroom when I couldn't read a paragraph.

My sisters and I were the only Indian children at Whittier Elementary School. It was hard anyway just to be living in Mitchell because of the prejudice. Maybe that was why we were treated so disrespectfully in and out of school.

One teacher I had, made me feel dirty because of the dirt under my fingernails. She used her long fingernails to clean mine; it always hurt when she did this.

Another teacher, Ms. Gibson, stood five-foot-one. In a year, I would be as tall as her. She had glasses hanging from her neck. She wore thick black shoes. Her walk was heavy, her shoes loud. She wore dark dresses with belts. She was a mean little woman who didn't care for Indians. I could feel that in her attitude and the rude way she spoke to me. When I had a hard time pronouncing a word that didn't come out right or sound right, and I didn't continue reading, she loudly remarked, "You're going to grow up to be dumb Indian. Doesn't your mother help you read at home?"

I didn't say anything. I just put my head down on the desk.

One time in class I asked her permission to go to the bathroom. I had a stomach flu. She said I should have gone before class. Not feeling well, I asked again, and she loudly said, "No! You can wait."

I started to cry. The other kids were laughing, which made me more ashamed.

It was not my fault that I soiled myself, yet she made me feel that way. She grabbed me by the sleeve and dragged me to the restroom. She was an adult bully.

I wished I could disappear. I was so hurt, asking myself, *Why did this happen*? I wished someone could tell this teacher she will be punished.

Our mother wanted us to be safe, not be harmed in the town where we lived. My parents always encouraged my sisters and me to have confidence and self-esteem growing up, but we learned to be on high alert, scared of how we might be treated by the White community. Knowing at an early age how to think "just in case" helped me survive the boarding school treatment I would later navigate.

School wasn't bad at the beginning. My sisters and I got along with the White kids. We all played together. But the way we were treated became increasingly confusing and scary. We learned quickly about racism, living with caution and being careful where we went. My parents were afraid we would get hurt, beat up. I guess we were targets to be bullied; we weren't street smart.

My father had strong respect for women; we were all girls. He wanted to protect us from the offensive, derogatory words toward Indian women that were hurtful and degrading. My mother warned us that if any taunting or racist name-calling happened to us on our way home from school, we were to walk across the street or ignore it.

But ignoring it didn't change anything. We were called sexual words, and coins were thrown at us. We just kept walking. I assumed this was only in Mitchell; I thought it was the only racist place where Indian people were treated so badly. The all-White community yelled unkind remarks such as, "You dirty Indian squaw, you are only good for one thing, sex, you drunk Indian."

The cruel words hurt. Confused at first, I thought the verbal attacks were personal—did I do something to offend someone? I finally realized the hate was for all my people. So I had to know where not to go, to keep away from the haters.

When we were picked on and called racial slurs while on the way to and from school, half the time, I didn't know what they really meant. I saw some of the reactions of White people taunting us, how angry they became, their faces turning red as they yelled, "Go back to the reservation!" Or another good one, "Go back where you came from!"

Question: "Where is that?"

I found it confusing to be judged by my darker skin color and called hateful names by people with pale white skin who spent so much time sunbathing. I often heard White girls talk about how tanned they got or still wanted to get.

I felt pain being left out at school or not invited to a classmate's birthday sleepover. I was the last to be picked for any game. I hated going to the playground where the opportunity was for the White kids to bully us with name-calling.

I was invited to my first birthday party by twin schoolmates, a brother and sister. I was happy to be invited, but I had no money to buy a big gift. I had two brand-new pencils that I had saved for a long time and never used. I wrapped them to give to the twins.

I felt so out of place at the party. I didn't fit, not knowing how to act. We played games, had cake and other food. Then it was time to open the presents. I was ashamed that my inexpensive gift wasn't like other kids' really nice gifts. I wished I could shrink, fall between cracks of the floor. I just wanted to leave. I was happy when the party was finally over. I couldn't wait to go home. The next school day one of the girls who was at the party told me the twins "had to" invite me; their mother made them. That made the whole experience worse, thinking I was a pity invite. I can't see it any different way.

I enjoyed walking to school by myself. The walk was long from home to school. A special memory that makes me smile was when I sometimes stopped at a corner store on the way to school to buy penny candy. I had a dime or a nickel, a lot of money then. Some candy was two for a penny, which made my day better. I hid the candy from the teacher, otherwise she would take it away.

After school was the worst of being made fun of and called names. I rushed home. I liked being by myself; it was better. I avoided the trouble of kids who pretended they wanted to be friends. I never trusted anyone if I went anywhere downtown or after school.

Back then, I was not old enough to really understand what the word "prejudice" meant. I questioned many things, wanting to know why this happens.

I began to wonder, *Are all people like the people here?*

In those little White towns around the reservation, even my elders were discriminated against and treated badly. Often it was due to the language barrier. Most only spoke Dakota/Lakota or broken English, and they couldn't pronounce the English words.

Having both parents fluent in our original language, I had no problem understanding what was being asked or said. I often wondered when my mother or father looked puzzled while having to do any kind of business with the English language. No one helped translate for us. In those days, the English speakers frowned and made fun of us, shamed us, and told us we couldn't speak our language. We were made to learn and only speak English.

I knew in my heart I was proud to be Indian. I came from the original people who were proud people, who lived by the values of caring for each other. I saw this in the way my father carried himself with pride even when the name-calling started in town, people "whooping" at him and calling him "Chief." He never hung his head in shame. But hearing harassment on a daily basis, can make a person start to feel inferior. People in the non-Indian community gave that stare, then they stepped away, keeping a distance. I hated that stare, and that look away.

I ask myself now, *Why do I keep those bad times in my thoughts?*

Not all the people in Mitchell were unkind. I had a teacher who was a kind, patient, White lady. She spent extra time helping me with school work, which was another way to get attention from her. She made me feel special. She never embarrassed me or shamed me in front of the class. When I turned twelve, I had a birthday cake for the first time. It came from my teacher. The most beautiful lemon cake with yellow frosting flowers, a big "Happy Birthday" on top, and a card too. The writing in the card said I was "special" and to have "many more to come." I was so proud and happy to get that cake and a dollar card. I couldn't wait to get home to show Mom and Daddy.

I don't remember ever having cake in our home. I guess we were more traditional. I got the strong message from my parents that celebrating birthdays with a cake was a White man's way. We celebrated other things in life, like what we accomplished, usually with a feast with relatives. Everyone was welcome. Just come and eat. The biggest honor I knew of was to earn an eagle feather or plume and be given your Indian name.

My dream would have been to stay in the tiospaya where we grew up, rather than living where we weren't wanted. I never wanted to be discriminated against, looked upon as filthy disgusting human being who doesn't belong there. I'd like never to experience the racist remarks. But our family couldn't go back to the reservation. There was no housing or jobs that my father could have. My sisters and I were rushed into learning how to get used to a place we weren't really part of. We had to assimilate. Being poor wasn't a choice for my father or others who wanted to provide for their families. Over time my sisters and I learned how to adapt and, most importantly, to keep safe from harm.

Chapter 3

For Our Own Good

In 1967 I was twelve when our family was visited by a white-haired lady they called Mrs. Wood, a county health nurse. She was short, chubby, and dressed in an all-White nurse uniform. Her hat had a red cross in the front. She smelled like antiseptic. She had short fat legs; her ankles looked like white sponges hanging over her white shoes.

Who was this person?

Somehow this White county nurse "convinced" my parents to send me and my four little sisters away "for our own good" to Marty, the St. Paul's Indian Mission Boarding School near the Missouri River, about seventy miles south of our family home in Mitchell. That nurse thought she was doing my family a favor, wanting to save us "poor little Indian kids."

From who? From what?

On a day in early September, my sisters and I were waiting to start a new school year at Whittier Elementary School. But instead, a thin, White social worker picked up my four younger sisters and me to take us to Marty. We had no control over what was happening to us. We were all put in the car, puzzled, not knowing where we were going.

I don't know what was said that day, but we were offered no explanation for why we were being taken away at the time, even from our parents. My sisters and I had to come up with our own ideas about the reason. We only learned much later that our parents were given no choice. In fact, they were threatened and told their daughters would be taken away from them if they did not send five of us to Marty—me and my four little sisters. The youngest was six. I am sure this was an emotional hardship for my parents.

I remember the look on each of my little sisters' faces, their scared blank stares. I felt the same in silence. Inside I cried and begged. We didn't want to go. I wanted to stay home. In slow motion, we were all put in the car, feeling scared and confused, wondering where we were going. Next came the longest ride of our lifetime.

My little sisters cried quietly. I refused to cry or show any feeling. I couldn't, otherwise I knew it would be worse for my sisters. I had to be strong. I had no power to do or say anything.

I still have a vivid picture in my mind of that first time approaching the boarding school run by the Catholic Church. The long road there was up a small hill, just high enough to see a church steeple in the distance. As we came closer to the school, it felt dark and lonely. All I could see were cold, empty fields, a few houses here and there. Nothing else.

We sat quietly, not saying a thing, feeling all the heaviness of being alone. My little sisters sat very close to one another. I heard a small whine as they tried to hide their sniffling. It was so hard not to cry, seeing their fear and sadness. I wanted them to feel safe, not to be sad.

I'm here with you. I huddled close to my little sisters. We didn't know what was going to happen next. I thought if we were together it wouldn't be so bad.

The social worker left us at Marty without saying anything to us, nothing at all. She just drove off. I will never forget that day. I was so upset that I didn't really notice who met us there. All the adults I saw that day wore long black clothes with half of their faces covered. I had never seen a nun before.

My heart was beating so fast as it became clear that I was being separated from my little sisters. We were abandoned, told nothing, still given no explanation as to why we were there, or when we would go home. We had never been apart, not ever.

By then I was crying. No one asked, "Are you okay?"

I felt hurt and mad at anyone who had a part of this happening to me. I hated my mother too. *Why did she do this to her daughters?*

Even now as an adult, thinking of that day, I suddenly feel like that little girl. Taken by surprise yet again, I regress. I have to stop for a few minutes to regain my thoughts. I have stuffed those negative thoughts so deep inside. I never wanted to reopen them and remember how cruel that place was.

~

Without explanation, a woman in black took me away from my sisters and into the St. Theresa building. Every building at Marty was named after a saint. All the buildings had big windows. Almost immediately, the woman in black began talking about all the rules I must obey.

The first floor of the St. Theresa building was a laundry room with ironing boards and a cleaning closet with mops, pails, and brooms. A large mostly empty room was called the Rec Room. The second floor was the school from kindergarten to eighth grade.

My bed was on the third floor with the big girls (seventh and eighth graders) and one nun. I was placed into seventh grade. My four little sisters were all placed in another part of the same building, the other half of the third floor.

My bed was in the middle of a row of metal-framed beds; the other side of the room was set up the same. Each girl was assigned a single bed with a pillow, two white sheets, and a dark-green wool army blanket. We had to make our bed with all the sides tucked in tightly, or we had to make it over. We had a small box at the end of the bed where we kept personal stuff—everything we owned, which wasn't much of anything. We came to Marty without clothes other than what we wore. That was one reason we didn't expect to be staying very long. We were unaware that leaving everything about our former lives at home was part of the plan. We had nothing to remind us of the home left behind, just our childhood memories. We were given clothes that were donated to the Church.

The nun's room was to one side of the space, and just inside the nun's room was a door connecting to the little girls' dorm. In the center was another double door between the two dorms. In the evening I could sometimes hear the little girls playing and laughing; often I wondered if that was one of my sisters. I missed them so much. I just wanted to be with them and feel safe with my family. I was used to being with all my sisters in one fairly small space and doing everything together. I was thinking that after we settled in, I could be with my sisters; but I didn't get to see them that often or even have a chance to play or talk to them. I saw them only in passing. That separation was the hardest part for me.

My youngest sister had been put into kindergarten and almost immediately became very sick and cried all the time. My mother came and picked her up. I wasn't allowed to ask about or see her; I didn't know why she was going home. Maybe she got sick from being separated from our parents for the very first time. All we knew was that she was sent home.

Every part of our life was controlled by the Church. I really didn't understand why we were disciplined so severely. The nuns and priests used harsh methods to correct any behavior—slapping, hitting, and other mistreatments.

I remember all the negative incidents. They became part of me, like a blueprint of a hidden, forgotten little girl who would turn into a hurt, sad adult forever. I remember it like a nightmare. We could always hear the dorm nun and the other nuns coming because of the rattling of their rosary beads and the heavy keys they carried on their sides.

Father Cashmere was a tall man who wore a white beanie on his head and dressed all in white. I was with another student one day walking behind "the father"; I was laughing with this other girl. To this day I don't know why he turned around and slapped me hard with an open hand. The priest didn't stop to tell me what I did wrong; he just went on his way. Scared, I wondered what I should do. I knew we couldn't talk back to any adult. I never thought that hitting a little girl was okay. I felt so embarrassed, ashamed, like it was my fault. I must have caused it. But nothing was said. I had a big red mark left on my cheek that stung and felt hot most of the day.

Punishment continued as if it was a normal thing, like brushing our teeth every morning. I figured the other kids must not care. They didn't say much about what was going on, everyone just complied, as though they were fine. Is that how it looks to be controlled?

I guessed they knew the strict schedule and just got along, knowing what to do: the chores, when to eat, sleep, go to mass. The routine was the same every day.

I found it hard to get used to living in a dorm. I was told what to do, what to believe. And every time I was corrected meant being slapped, hit, beaten, and/or belittled. There was no one to complain to or go to for comfort.

Before long, whatever discipline of other children (actually abuse) was not hidden from us, it was done right in front of us. It didn't concern the adult who was doing the discipline; they obviously never gave a thought or a care about how their mistreatment might affect us all emotionally.

Seeing violent abuse like this toward others made us afraid for ourselves; we all kept very quiet. We felt powerless. We were so young. We weren't mature enough to understand how wrong all of this was.

I knew my little sisters hurt as much as I did. They went through more feelings of being abandoned so young. At least they had each other. My next youngest sister became the protector; she was nurturing to the younger ones.

Beyond missing them, I was homesick. nothing made me happy there.

Thinking back, I can still hear the windows howl, a creepy whistling sound from the wind blowing on cold dark nights. At night we only see dim lights from the buildings. It was the loneliest place, and the lonely feeling was the worst I ever knew as a child. I was by myself. My sisters and I were isolated, and under the complete control of the (all-White) nuns and priest at Marty. Our parents could not even afford to visit us.

Looking out the big windows in my dorm, I could see the empty, flat farm fields for miles, nothing but emptiness outside, just the wind blowing, sometimes tossing around a tumbleweed. It appeared happy just rolling around, but I felt all alone not being with my sisters. I often daydreamt staring out the window, thinking, *If we were home, I wouldn't feel this way*.

I was so alone and depressed. The lonesome sound of the wind whistling through the cracks in the tall window kept me awake and wishing I could go home. The students who lived locally usually went home on holidays. That was an especially lonely time, having to stay as others went home.

I felt abandoned by the people who loved me. I was separated from my home. I was sad for my little sisters not seeing our mother, not being home.

I wondered if our mother was thinking about us, was she looking forward to seeing us, was she coming to get us, or see us? No one contacted us to tell us we would be going home for the holidays. We had to stay once again.

I was so angry at my mother. It didn't make any sense. How can anyone leave their children? *Who does that?* I was so angry, knowing I was left there to stay. I hated everything about the place. I was lonesome and bitter. I had to always be vigilant, on alert for the arbitrary punishment from the nuns or a priest.

I promised myself, *I will leave this horrible place.*

I kept telling myself, *I will not cry.*

~

Most of the students who attended BIA mission boarding schools lived in the local areas surrounding the reservation. The schools did not provide traditional book learning. Instead, boys were taught common labor work on farms, and girls were taught household chores, sewing, and cleaning. We had a schedule for each day of the week that included daily mass and assigned chores. Every day was the same, with nothing to look forward to.

The same routine took time to get used to. The nun got us up before it was light out, to hurry to get ourselves ready for the day, brush our teeth, comb our hair, make sure our face was clean, and get dressed. We had to make our bed a certain way, tightly tucked, with the pillow neatly at the head of the bed.

Before breakfast, we had to go to the church for mass from 6:00 to 7:00 a.m. On the way, we had to follow the nun who "watched over" the dorm. She (Sister B) was the meanest cruel person. She must have hated taking care of children. She was an adult and a bully. We had to make sure we didn't wander outside the boundary lines on the way to church.

Entering the church, the sound was hollow. You could hear voice echoes, we had to whisper, stay quiet, be still. The huge church was a cold, dark, unloving place that smelled bad at mass time. We had to make sure we covered our heads. Entering through the church door, we had to put our fingers in a bowl of water and make a sign of the cross.

We had to kneel before we sat down. Then a whole hour of repeating the same words over and over, while the stuff they burned smelled awful on an empty stomach.

Because I wasn't Catholic, I wasn't allowed to go near certain little rooms or go to the front and get the small, thin white wafers. After mass was benediction, and prayer for my sins. Praying for half an hour seemed like forever. Not knowing any better, I thought I must have a lot of sins that needed to be forgiven. I prayed not to go into that church ever again, but we went to mass every morning.

Marty was rigid, demanding. The students did all the cleaning. We were assigned chores. I had the kitchen. Breakfast was at 8:00 a.m., then kitchen duty. My chores were loading the dishwasher with silverware, drying them, and putting them away. To this day, I hate washing silverware, remembering those times. There wasn't a training period. We were only shown once what to do. We had to learn quickly. I dared not to ask the dorm nun to show me anything one more time, unless I wanted to hear her loud mean voice. I thought it was better to pretend and learn by watching the other girls do their chores. I got it down quickly, but I resented the way she treated all of us. She was a bully. Obedience was enforced with physical violence, inflicting pain. We had the option to obey all the rules or refuse and suffer the consequences of punishment. There was no rule against beating, hitting, or slapping. Leaving marks was not allowed, so no one would see bruises if we left the grounds. I couldn't tell whether the person who did the discipline was in a bad or good mood.

Once chores were done, we had free time to go outside. No special activities to do, we just had to stay outside. This was the only time I saw my little sisters—only I couldn't get close to them; I had to make sure I didn't get them or myself into trouble. They had strict boundaries too. They had to stay at the end of their dorm, or they would be punished harshly, even though they were so much younger. We all had to stay outside until the nun unlocked and opened the door to start school.

If I could have seen my sisters more, if we could be in the same dorm, maybe the adjustment would not have been so hard. We would have been able to support and take care of each other. I could have made sure nothing bad happened to them. I was glad they at least had each other.

At lunch time we had an assigned seating arrangement. The "big girls" were at one table, big boys on another side, the "little girls" at another table. I could only see my sisters eat from a distance. The high school students all sat at their own tables across the room.

Mealtimes had strict rules too. The nuns served the food. We had to keep our elbows down by our sides, and don't dare ever put them on the table. Dare not talk back, and it was too bad if you didn't like the food. The rule was to eat everything they put on your tray, otherwise, the nun shouted at me. It was embarrassing. Over time, I learned to eat the food and remembered not to put my elbows on the table while eating.

If you threw up, you were the one to clean it up. One time we were given corn bread and honey that had bees' body parts. They raised bees I guess and didn't clean the honey too well. That honey full of bee body parts was the only sweet thing we ever had.

If anyone disobeyed or broke a rule, they might not get to eat at all. By the time the dorm nun did that to me, I didn't care. Each day I was becoming more stubborn, hardened. My only thought was to get expelled and go home. Every time she approached me with a new way to punish me, I pretended I didn't care. She was mean either way. Mostly it was hurtful shaming.

I missed home where we just had one rule: take enough food to eat, and don't waste food. In my community I was taught that we each have our own talents, and that I was a gift from the Creator. That was the community I once had, a long time ago. Now I had to learn to endure the pain of the message I got at Marty: "Go away. You're nobody, not special. You're not an individual; don't be Indian."

I had to learn how to turn off that voice inside my head and fill my thoughts with silence, place myself somewhere else to endure abuse. Never once did anyone come to rescue me.

I felt powerless. No one ever explained what was going to happen next. I often wondered, *What is going to happen? Who am I?*

One cold night, as I was looking out of the large window in the dorm after it had snowed for a few days, the snow was packed down hard. It seemed like the wind was picking up small sparks in the snow, like me wanting to be carried away by the wind. On that loneliest night, I felt crushed by abandonment—*did my parents really agree and allow this to happen?*

The nuns and their Church controlled every move we made—with a lot of restrictions, and their generous daily practice of corporal punishment for any of our deviation from their rules. We were either locked out or locked up. Free time indoors was the Rec Room where there was nothing to play with, only a few chairs and a Bible. We couldn't go beyond the invisible boundaries. Planned fun was never heard of, there was no leaving the school just to do something different. We had to stay at Marty year-round. Breakfast, lunch, supper, chores, mass, and school were all the same, seven days a week. I wasn't in jail, but I was confined.

Summers were quiet, lonesome, in a dead place, an empty time space that felt like it would go on forever. Same as the holiday breaks, our parents never came, and we had to stay put. A few other students stayed back too. Most Indian families didn't have much money—just enough to survive day to day. I understood that we were poor; our parents couldn't afford to come to get us. We never had a phone or a good running car, let alone gas money. School was a long way from Mitchell.

My life moved in slow motion in that dark, cold place. I was so homesick, I felt sick. I despised every moment I was there. Everything reminded me that I was not home.

Will I ever be home?

I will not make friends be quiet, stay by myself. I just want to disappear, be invisible. I have to find ways to cope. I just have to make through another day and avoid the dorm nun.

I will try to go home. I will run away.

All I wanted was to go home, but I didn't even know which way to go. I tried my best to be suspended. The blueprint of my inner spirit was a golden-brown Indian girl who was forever sad.

Marty boarding school didn't have a good academic program. I went to classes, barely. School was really difficult for me. I know the Catholic rituals upside-down and sideways, but I didn't understand the things we were being taught. I was behind academically and struggled to catch up. Book learning was taught through the three R's, with no interaction between teacher and student. I had to pretend I was learning, not wanting to be found out.

The Catholic school taught no compassion for the human being. It demanded conforming to strict rules and the Church was the disciplinarian. Not having an adult to protect me made me become a needy child, suffering, having no sense of connection, shutting down, not saying much, only speaking when the nun called on me. Otherwise I didn't want any part of this. I was thinking that whatever happened to me, it wouldn't matter. I was that little Indian girl with dark-brown skin, sitting in the playground, looking up at the sky and clouds, wondering if Mom or Daddy was looking up too, and wondering how I was, or if they missed me like I missed them.

I cried because I hated the nuns, priest, fathers, whatever they call themselves. All I knew was that their God was mean, because they beat me with belts or with their hands, then turned around and asked me to say "this many" Hail Marys, because I was going to burn in hell.

To me, I was in hell already.

Chapter 4

My Bully & Sister B

I wasn't at Marty very long before an older Indian girl decided she didn't like me, and she started to bully me. I didn't know her. She had two girls who always hung around her, like sidekicks. She often recruited other girls to do all the hitting and pushing. She was never alone when she had anything mean to say. She told others what to do, while she stood on the sidelines, saying awful things about me.

It was hard to understand why any Indian girl wanted to bully me. I was Indian too. I had experienced being called names in elementary school in Mitchell, but no one dared to hit us. Her bullying included being jumped and hit by the bully's' flunkies. She lived locally, so I couldn't wait for this bully to go home for the holidays. I wouldn't have terrible thoughts and worry about what was going to happen next, be called names or be pushed and hit.

I wasn't familiar with the particular racist names the bully called me. She said I was a "nigger Indian with big lips." I'd never heard that "insult" before. I had a golden-brown skin color and long black hair. Color issues weren't part of my growing up Indian. I thought the only difference in Indians was that you came from different tribes. I didn't know what a Black person was; the town where I grew up had no Black families. I'd never heard a single racial slur come from my parents or other family members' mouths, even when White people called my parents racist names. It took me by surprise that another Indian could be mean and prejudiced to her own kind. I thought only White people did that sort of name calling.

The lesson my bully was teaching me back then was to hate who I was, be ashamed of being "Indian." I was no good, a nothing. The ugly words she said made me feel like I must be ugly.

The bully's words haunted me after a while. I had to be on high alert, fearing the worst at any time. Being bullied was a nightmare that didn't stop. I told the dorm nun about this girl picking on me. She always said, "Stop lying, don't be tattletale," so I stopped telling her anything. I learned quickly never to talk openly about how I was being treated.

The dorm nun herself abused girls physically and verbally, but she had her favorites. The bully had to be the nun's pet. She never got in trouble for bullying me. I felt I was singled out because the values I was taught at home were so different. I didn't fit in; I was quiet.

On a day when one of the older girls had her period, the dorm nun was so angry, demanding, "Who didn't dispose of their pad properly?"

For once I knew it wasn't me going to get in trouble or blamed. I was too young to have a period, *what a relief*. She talked like all girls were nasty. In my tiospaya, my female relatives had told me to take care of my body, that I would soon enter another season of being a woman, but this dorm nun made us feel like being female was dirty, nasty, unclean.

No one volunteered to step forward to take the blame. No one said anything; we all knew better.

The nun was annoyed, angry. She hollered so loud, "If you don't tell me, everyone will be punished."

When we all remained silent, she made all of us kneel on a cold, hard concrete floor. We all kneeled. It seemed like forever before we were allowed to stand up and go to bed. My knees were cold and had a red mark from kneeling that turned into a bruise the next day.

Nothing was said, it was another normal day, like always.

~

I had to learn how to protect myself from the nun's pet. I thought it was better to keep to myself, but not to be caught by myself. Ignoring her didn't work. The bullying continued. She was mean and sneaky. Bullies can be very creative in coming up with ways to pick on you without getting caught. She was good at having others do the hitting or bullying. One time I was pushed hard from behind when we were lined up to go into the cafeteria. I couldn't catch my balance in my fall. I hit the wall and got a big bump on my forehead. It hurt, but what hurt more was the laughing and being shamed in front of everyone else.

I was confused. *Why is this happening?*

I want to go home. I want to go home. I want to go home.

I learned to escape by disconnecting, putting myself somewhere in order not to *feel.* I kept repeating to myself, *Nothing will last forever.* Doing this helped me deal with the abuse at the moment it was happening. I told myself this to believe *I'm in a safe place* until it was over.

One Saturday, while I was doing chores, cleaning the bathroom floor tile, I tried to hurry up and get done, because I was by myself that day. The bully cornered me. Instantly my stomach hurt. I was breathing hard, and trying to control my breaths so she wouldn't notice and know I was scared of her.

She tried to convince me to go with her, she had "something to show" me. I told her no. I knew she was lying and up to no good because she was being too nice to me. She was never nice to me. She was also never alone; she was always with other girls. I knew she only wanted to make my life miserable.

She kept saying, "I won't do anything to you, just come with me."

I figured that, either way, she was going to push me, pull my hair, and call me names. I thought maybe she was going to fight me.

I thought, *I hate you, let's get this over with.*

I followed her down to the Rec Room, knowing it wouldn't be good. I became more frightened the closer we came to the room. I felt frozen in time and space as five girls circled around me. They pushed me up against a wall so I couldn't get away, while punching me and pulling my hair. Their taunting voices sounded so far away. I blocked out the pain so it wouldn't hurt when it came.

I felt something hot on my arm. The bully had a pocket knife that she scraped on the cement wall to make it hot. Then all the girls gathered around me. I had no choice but to stand still. I was able to hold back my tears; I would not give them the pleasure to see me cry or beg them to let me go. I stood there watching, wondering who's gonna hit me first, when they all came at me at once.

I just got fed up. This had to stop. *Either I do something, or I get beat up.*

I was able to grab one of the girls by the back of her hair. The other girls hit and kicked me while they giggled and laughed. I got real angry, fighting back, punching, and pulling the one girl's hair. I had to show them I wasn't scared, that I would protect myself even when outnumbered. I hoped she would go to that horrible place called Hell.

As I held back my tears and showed no emotion, this was the first time I left my body. I looked up. I heard voices outside the big windows. Then I saw one of my little sisters looking in the window. She was crying. I saw her look, so helpless. It reminded me of the first day we were dropped off here, feeling helpless, alone. Seeing her, I felt so helpless and bad. Seeing her crying made me sad. She witnessed the fight.

I didn't care if I was hurt with bruises. I just didn't want her to feel bad or to get into a fight with one of the girls. I wanted to let my little sister know that I wasn't hurt, I didn't want her to feel bad about me. I couldn't comfort her. I became even more angry. I hated this place. I despised the bully more because she made my little sister cry.

Suddenly the lookout girls said someone was coming, and the girls dispersed.

The bully made my life a living hell. I wished she would go there and burn up. I wished karma would come back and hurt this person just like I was hurt.

The only single thing I had control over was a thought, a promise I made: From that day on, I decided I would never show my true emotions. I would never let the bully see me cry, even if she and her girls hurt me physically, leaving bruises.

I got good at blocking out pain. Painful memories made me cry only when I was alone. Otherwise I swallowed it, making that big lump go down.

What had hurt me the most that day was seeing my little sister crying, seeing me attacked. Through the window, I saw her pain in her face. She was too young; she didn't understand what was going on.

Feeling depressed and trapped helped me perfect a new behavior: leaving my body when I was physically abused, always making sure not to let anyone know that it hurt. I learned to shut down. I got real good at shutting down. It was like a black out. I could leave my body when I was being hurt.

Meanwhile, I had to find a way to get expelled from this place. I asked around whether other kids had ever been expelled or suspended for running away or getting caught smoking.

I will run away, and go home, then I will come for my sisters.

~

I ran away in the late fall, but I never made it home. I didn't really know which way to go. I had to walk. It was cold, close to winter. I knew my grandparents lived south. If I could go there, I'd be safe, maybe they would take me back home.

It turned out they weren't home, and it was getting dark.

What should I do now?

I didn't want to go back. I knew I would get punished, be hit or whipped.

When I left, I didn't care. I just wanted to leave. I hated this place so much; I'd never experienced this kind of treatment. We were never punished like that at home.

I decided to stay in the barn that night. The only company I had were chickens. The barn did stop the cold wind; but it was still cold. I had matches, but I don't remember where I got them. I'd seen my father build a fire for my mother to cook back when we lived in a tent. Those days were my happiest times as a young child.

I put some hay in a small pile in the corner of the barn and tried to light it with a match. The flames didn't look like what I remembered, and I was afraid I would burn down my grandparents' barn. I was really lucky I was able to put out the fire.

Seeing the hens clucking loud, running everywhere in the barn—I learned from that experience to never try something until you understand what you're doing. Respect the fire.

I was so cold. I still didn't want to go back to Marty. I left the barn, not knowing where to go.

I saw a small white house across the field. I didn't know the people, or if anyone still lived there. I walked up to the door and knocked, hoping someone was home. An Indian lady answered. She must have known I was from the school. She invited me in.

Her home was warm from a wood-burning stove. She cooked some fry bread. It was hot, it tasted so good.

She asked if I came from Marty, and I answered yes. She asked if the school knew where I was. She asked if I ran away.

I nodded my head, *yes*.

While I was eating, she told me I should go back, that they may be worried about me. She told me I could spend the night, but then I would have to go back.

I knew the school wasn't worried or looking for me. The dorm nun would know I was gone when she did the bed check. The dorm doors would be locked.

Running away didn't work. I had to return to Marty.

I went back.

I was scared of the dorm nun. *What was going to happen?*

She didn't say much to me. The day went on like any other normal day. But that night I was punished for running away. She told me I had to go through the "belt line."

I didn't know what this meant.

She yelled for the older girls to line up in a row on two sides. She instructed the girls that they could hit and punch me below my neck, and not my face. They were only allowed to use their fists, no kicking.

Then she stood in front of the line and told me I had to walk between the lines of the girls, and I couldn't run or fight back. I had to walk slowly. I had to walk slowly or be made to go through the belt line again.

I had no choice but to do it, but it was the longest walk. It seemed like forever. All I saw was the shadow of the older girls' fists, and I heard their laughter. The girls used their fists to slug me from both sides. I felt so helpless, wishing I could die.

I close my eyes tight. *Don't cry. Don't cry.*

I tried to block the pain; I put my arms across my stomach.

The belt line taught me to hate the girls. I wished the nun would get into trouble and be beaten just the way I was that night.

I didn't say a word when it was over. I went to bed. Then I cried quietly, making sure no one could hear me. The bruises all the way down my arm were dark blue and black.

I heard the girls' laughter the next morning.

That next day it seemed like nothing happened. That wasn't the first or the last time being punished. Nor was that the only time I was punished by that nun.

I knew I was beginning to get on the dorm nun's nerves. I knew she didn't like me, and I didn't care for her. She lost my respect the day she punished me in the way she did. I didn't care anymore if she was irritated. I didn't jump like the rest of the students. I just took my time. She couldn't punish me, because I was obeying.

I got used to hearing her shaming words and put downs, but I was tired of being treated badly; the hitting, the belt lines, the kneeling. I usually just stood there, wanting it to get it over with quickly. No adult was there to rescue me.

After a while I was so mad, I made up my mind that I would not listen to anyone. Each day I become more stubborn. I kept quiet, not talking at all. It was my way of shutting down. I dreamt and hoped to go home, whatever it takes.

All I wanted was to go home. I want to be expelled and sent home.

I tried doing everything I was told not to do, thinking if I did so I would be sent home. The goal was to get home. I tried everything I had heard about or could come up with to be expelled. I heard many of the girls say you could be expelled for smoking.

Thinking they would have to get in touch with my mother to come after me, then my little sisters, I purposely got caught smoking.

The dorm nun pulled me by my arm to her bathroom and made me sit on the side of the tub. She took a cigarette and slowly ripped it apart. "Here, eat this."

At first I resisted; I just held my head down. She pulled my head up hard by my long hair.

She yelled, "Eat it. You're not leaving this room until you eat it up."

She told me not to spit it out.

Tears felt hot rolling down my face, but I refused to sob. I took the cigarette, put it in my mouth, chewing slowly. I was gagging, and I wanted to throw up.

She grabbed my hair again and said, "Eat it! Don't spit it out, swallow!"

I slowly ate the tobacco. The taste was awful. I couldn't swallow it down. It came back up, and she made me swallow my vomit. I had to make it stay down.

She finally said, “Go!”

It was over. Despising her more, I left her room. I felt sick to my stomach. I threw up my supper and the tobacco too. I will never forget that taste or how my throat hurt from trying to keep the tobacco down. I still remember how she looked, how her voice sounded.

She told me, “Be quiet.” She told me that telling anyone about it wouldn’t matter, because I didn’t matter.

This was the dorm nun who “took care” of us.

Now I was more determined to go home.

~

From what I could see, this White man’s Catholic Church was cruel and dark. The nuns and priests presented themselves as if they cared for and loved each child, as though they were looking out for each of us. But they showed that “love” by hitting us, beating us down, manipulating our thinking, and saying that everything bad that happened was our fault.

The nuns said our traditional beliefs were wrong, and how we prayed was with evil, devil words. I was judged wrong just for being myself.

Their God did not care about me. I wasn’t safe or protected. This was not the love I was taught at home. All I knew was that I was in an awful, scary place. No one took the time to explain who or what this man was who dressed in a white robe and hung on a cross, with the saddest look on his face. I couldn’t make sense of what I was told about this religion. I was confused when they preached that this Jesus was a loving man who died for our sins.

I was puzzled. *Why would Jesus die for me? What or who really was this person they called Jesus? Was he that “loving” god?*

Though I heard over and over that Jesus loved me and died for me, through my eyes, he was a mean, unloving person who must hate children. What else could it be? The nuns never said anything different, so that was true as I saw it. I could not fully understand the mixed message of a religion that talked about loving you one day and then punished you harshly the next if I didn’t believe and obey whatever I was told.

The White man's religion pretty much convinced me that I was the sinner, living in sin. I was going to hell. The nuns repeated this on a daily basis. I couldn't get away from it. At mass twice a day plus Sunday and from each priest and nun, they drilled the same message into my head. I had to "eat the body and drink the blood of Jesus," and pray to have my sins forgiven.

My spirituality, what I believed before coming to Marty, was nothing like this Catholic Church. This was weird and scary to me, causing me to mistrust, twist, and confuse my thinking about a loving God.

If God loved me, why wouldn't he protect me from the nuns and the girls who bullied me?

Besides, I was lied to. The nuns said that if I prayed "real hard" and asked for forgiveness, all my other prayers would be answered. I kneeled and prayed, but my prayers were never answered, because I was still here. I just wanted to go home.

Why are we being kept here this long? I wondered, *What is wrong with me?*

"They" were the evil ones for wanting to convert and change our way of thinking, destroy our beliefs, and take away all my Indian core values. That distorted message while living in the two chaotic worlds damaged many young children's minds, causing so much confusion even later in life.

Who am I? Where do I belong? Where do I go from here? Is it because I didn't pray hard enough to be forgiven that I'm having such a hard time?

In a conversation with one of my sisters many years later, mentioning the boarding school, we asked each other, "Where's purgatory?"

Are we there now?

We laughed, remembering they told us we were going to this place because of our sins. We agreed that the priest and nuns should have gone there for *their* sins! They were the worst sinners. They took the dollars they received for each Indian child at the school, taken so far away from their family. They kept control and isolated the parents, even discouraging parents to visit their children. The entire church and school experience seemed designed to destroy our self-esteem, damage us children, and devastate our family dignity just for being Indian—people they considered uncivilized savages. Where did these values come from? Why did we have to accept another man's ways and beliefs?

I felt the Church was awful, and God was watching me.

Day by day, I began to not like myself.

I felt like a nothing.

At some point, I made up my mind that I wouldn't believe in the Catholic Church's ways.

Chapter 5

Home

I finally just walked out of Marty, taking the raw emotion with me and thinking, *I will be alright when I'm home.* I wanted to be told I wasn't abandoned. I wanted an explanation for why we were sent to Marty in the first place.

And for once in a long time, I felt happy. I was home. At first it seemed like nothing had happened, as though I was always home. But the feeling in the house was different. It didn't feel welcoming. My parents were strangers. I had to get reacquainted with my mother. She wasn't the same person she was when we left. She was distant. I kept asking when the rest of my sisters would come home. She didn't answer any of my questions. She just looked away. I felt like I was stuck in the same age I was when I got out of the car at Marty.

My father said he was glad I came home. But he wasn't living with my mother. That was strange. *What happened?* He seemed quieter, and appeared exhausted. Time had taken a toll on him. His fight was gone. He no longer wanted to deal with discrimination. He was struggling now with a developing drinking problem. I was sad to see this. He had gone through a lot in his lifetime; he was just tired. I had often heard him say he didn't want to live past fifty, he wanted to die before turning fifty. I always said, "Don't say that!"

As time went by at home, I wasn't as happy as I thought I would be. I wondered, *What's wrong with me? Wasn't going home what obsessed me day after day?*

I had enrolled in the local school, which was a condition of coming home. I told myself I will do better now, and I will never go back to

Marty again. But I missed my little sisters. I wished they were home with me. My two older sisters had already moved away from home, so I was there by myself, and we were all living different lives.

Home wasn't at all what I expected it to be; it wasn't home anymore, but Mitchell hadn't changed. The people were still prejudiced. I was the only Indian in the school. I felt out of place. It was hard to become friends with any of the other kids.

Fine, I thought. *So I don't have any friends. It's a lot better that way.* I was used to being by myself. I wasn't afraid to be by myself. I would not depend on anyone to survive.

Life went on for a while, but I didn't feel right. Something was wrong, but I couldn't put my finger on what it was. I continued to go to school, but I started losing interest. I couldn't get used to not being controlled by rules. I had gone from being where every single move I made was monitored, to having no rules and no boundaries. I guess being at Marty for so long, being constantly programmed to obey in order to avoid being punished had become so routine that my learned behavior had become ingrained. Now I had freedom. I was in control, but out of control. I could do almost anything without punishment. I could go anyplace, do almost anything. I began to run around doing things I was told not to do. I stayed out all night, and I tried alcohol. That was fun in the beginning, but I wasn't happy. I wasn't comfortable at home or at school.

I had depended most on my mother, but she was no longer like a parent. I observed how she wasn't home very much and was always on the go. She had built a new world without us kids. We were away so long that she was used to not having us around. She was no longer responsible for taking care of us. Seeing her living a single life, as though she was never a parent, made me angry. I wanted home to be the way it used to be.

My mother had gotten used to not having kids at home. She would go out drinking with her sister. I'd only see her for a short time just before my aunt picked her up. She was pretty, all dressed up like she was going somewhere special. She had lipstick on and wore perfume.

She never used to drink or go out at night. I knew not to ask her about it. She seemed angry. If I asked where she was going, she wouldn't say anything other than, "I'll be back."

I still had my father. I visited with him and stayed often at his place.

He lived in the same house my sisters and I were taken from. I didn't know or understand the reason my parents were distant from one another; they had always been together. Sadly, each one now made a life on their own. Not once did I ever hear my father say anything bad about my mother or blame her for any circumstances. He told me he didn't know why things turned out the way they did.

I thought maybe this was their way of adjusting to the circumstances forced on them. We had gone from our home without a hug or a kiss or anyone telling us not to worry or that they would come and get us.

I struggled each day at home where nothing was like the picture I had painted. Finally I knew I didn't want to stay home after all. I never would have dreamt I'd agree to go back to that place I despised, back to Marty. But now I was confused. I felt guilty, thinking, *How did it come to this? I want to go back to the place I hate?*

I had a plan that I would get my required education, then move on from there. So I asked my mother if she would talk to my uncle and auntie to see if I could stay with them and become day students at Marty. I would no longer be a boarder. If I wasn't a boarder, I wouldn't have to put up with bullies, the nun or the girl. I didn't know how it was going to turn out, but I needed to go back to school.

I was so happy my uncle and auntie said yes! I moved in right away. I had my own room and privacy. My cousins were younger than me. They were like little sisters plus one little baby brother. I became close to all of them. I love them now just like I did when I lived with them. My uncle and auntie were my parents. My auntie would not allow anything bad to happen to me. She was there to protect me and wouldn't let anyone hurt me again.

Going back there as a day student, I was allowed to go in the "big girls" door. I still saw that place as big and scary, and I told myself, *I will never step foot in that place ever.*

I was happy that I never had to deal with the bully, or the dorm nun, again. I didn't have to know either one of them. I felt good. I didn't have to go to Church, sit hour-long masses, praying in a way I didn't believe in.

I had Auntie and my uncle there who listened to me. I had always wished home was like this. If I was feeling bad or upset, I got encouragement from both of them.

The Indian boarding school wasn't any better this time around; bullies are everywhere. Being mean-spirited doesn't have a color label. My uncle told me not to be a resentful person because it could backfire. I was puzzled. I took his advice as saying it will work itself out.

I so loved my auntie; she was fun and funny. I loved her sense of humor. She loved to play tricks on me. One day when I got home after school, I asked where my uncle was. Auntie said he went out hunting. We visited and she asked me how school was. Then I went to my room to rest, and I fell asleep.

When I woke up, I turned, and on my pillow was the paw of a raccoon or squirrel. That scared me, but I knew Auntie put it there. I got up and found her and, when she looked at me, she started to laugh. She had a big heart. She always looked happy, she always made me smile. I felt good just being around her.

Uncle and Auntie both had my utmost respect. I felt so proud of them both. They encouraged me to go to college, envision a future, and consider helping "our people." They each did so much for me. I always wanted them to be proud of me.

At one point I told my uncle that I wanted to visit more colleges that weren't nearby.

He said, "That's good, my girl."

Not wanting to disrespect him by saying I did not want to go to college nearby in South Dakota, I said, "When I finish, maybe I could move back and help our people."

Surprised, Uncle said, "That's okay, maybe you could be somewhere else, helping other Indians."

I wholeheartedly heard this.

I learned some valuable lessons from my relatives, uncles and aunties. I knew I would have to work hard to survive, and that it would be important to give my children a home, not to be homeless like my mother experienced when she was a child. I was reminded to be grateful for having a home. Material objects come and can be gone the next day; anything you have can be taken. The value of money is to provide shelter, food, and the necessities to live. I can't miss something I never had. I don't know what it is to be privileged and not have to worry.

I had a grandma named Mabel, bless her soul. She was a beautiful, wise, elderly Indian woman whose skin was as dark as mine. I can't imagine how hard the discrimination she suffered must have been. She also lived off the reservation in a time when the prejudice was so much worse—up front in her face. I loved listening to stories about how she grew up and heard along the way, all the criticism for being an Indian woman.

I had another grandma named Rosie, bless her soul. She was a tall, dark-skin, elderly Indian woman of great pride, always neatly dressed. She wore red lipstick that made her skin color stand out more. Both these Indian women had dark golden-brown skin and beautiful lips shaped like hearts. Each carried themselves with the highest regard for being beautiful Indian women who didn't have to wear makeup. My grandma Rosie was sassy. I liked her spunk.

I had opportunities to listen and learn from these great elderly women who were strong and independent and never depended on anyone other than themselves. Both were beautiful women. I heard stories from each of them about the hard times in their lives. They were very grateful and thankful for what they had, and they did not seem angry or feel sorry for themselves for what they endured. I learned from these grandmothers that having a hard time is part of life, and it is up to me to decide how I'm going to live my life.

Both were independent. I asked each why they weren't married. Both had the same remark that they couldn't find a good Indian man anymore.

Why not? The answer was that they are dead. They knew how Indian men suffered the most from losing their role in society as strong warriors who were able to provide for their family.

My father, a strong Indian man, had suffered the White society deciding it would be better to exterminate his future offspring and kill off our race. Despite the racism and bad treatment in the White community, he never considered moving back to the reservation. We were the most happy together as a family.

My uncle and auntie always reassured me, "Have patience. Things will work out the way they are supposed to happen. Each day is new, and with patience we will be at peace, and our hearts will heal. Continue to be positive, live our life as such, with no regrets.

My uncle told me, "Yes it's hard, but all the power is here. No longer can anyone take your power or misuse you, Little Indian girl. Please smile, you already know the hard times and the pain of being alone."

I tried to hold on to these lessons. I still didn't believe in myself back then. But I felt strong, having faith I would find my way.

Chapter 6

Life After Marty

Indian people like me are still dealing with unresolved grief from being separated so young from family, the loss of childhood experiences, years in a Catholic boarding school, and having to deal with the multi-generational abuse of relatives who suffered more than I have. I read about the little children dying during the boarding school era. The schools didn't even inform the parents how or when their child had passed away. Just a small unmarked grave. My heart hurts for each child who wasn't honored, and for any parents who didn't know that their children died and were buried. I pray that God bless the souls of the many children who left too early at the hands of strangers.

The boarding schools "stole" children. No Indian parent would voluntarily give permission for their children to be taken far away from home to know the deep sadness, the ongoing homesickness, fear of being hit, beaten severely, abused again and again with no adult to protect from any harm or comfort them on the saddest days. All I knew was a sick feeling of sadness, emptiness, and the terror. *Will I (we) ever get to go home?*

Many more problems started for young people like me after leaving the boarding school, being broken and without future plans and without tools for dealing with the loss and pain we just wanted to forget. Many former students delved into negative, self-destructive behaviors, depression, drugs, alcohol, teen pregnancies, abusive relationships . . . the list goes on.

We didn't know what was missing or how much grief we held. We couldn't find any resources. Our tool boxes were empty, and we didn't have a clue what to do. I had so much to learn about becoming a young

Indian woman, without my role models to learn from. I didn't want to live some other way of life. I had to pretend I had assimilated to fit that mold.

The Church's influence continued to hold onto us. Something was wrong, broken. Having been conditioned, controlled, and brainwashed by the Church's authority and the ongoing abuse, I tried my best to catch up and grow up. Trying to figure out life was crazy-making, as I searched for someone or something to control or be controlled by. So much had already been taken from me and from the community I grew up in; I was lost in the big world. I knew nothing. I couldn't live in the moment, enjoy the hour or day.

The boarding school years took a toll on me over time. I didn't really notice that the past abuses followed me. It was inside me, but I didn't want to acknowledge it. Who would?

Neither I nor my four little sisters could ever forget how we were treated; it followed us in unhealthy ways throughout our lives.

True harmony wouldn't exist ever again for my family. I was broken, my little sisters would suffer as much as me. Being terrorized and bullied as a child caused stress in my life that came back in different forms, shapes, sounds, and smells. Hearing loud shouting triggered this fright mode "Don't hurt me," and fear came racing back. Hearing church bells triggered awful sadness and loneliness.

Whatever was healthy or harmful was unclear to me, or what I should to do next when warning signals went off. I felt I couldn't disagree or say the most important word, "No." I wasn't taught that I had the right to say no or to stand up for myself.

All my sisters became strong beautiful Indian women of all shades of color. Each sister was unique, very talented, and charming. We belonged together, were supposed to grow up together, know each other's hopes and dreams, and protect each other. Instead we grew up as strangers with the strong message that we weren't loved. Our "home" was torn apart and discarded, and we children were just thrown away like pieces of paper in the trash. We were physically kept away from each other, and cut off from our home, leaving many unanswered questions for a lifetime. The religious brainwashing abuse caused emotional trauma and stress disorder, suicidal thoughts, indifference to putting ourselves in danger.

Having our own families, and not being able to heal from the personal pain from the past, caused further stress and a tendency to overthink. Many times I had difficulty with my decision-making, and my critical thinking. I experienced confusion. Anxiety. When really bad, I had a panic attack that took my breath; I felt like everything was falling apart, I was overloaded. I experienced personal crises, but I couldn't understand that at the time.

I got mixed messages about where I might fit in. I was careful, observing who was around—something I learned at boarding school: stay alert to your surroundings. Never take anything for granted. (Laughing to myself now, I remember how I always tried to look up and look mad as a form of self-protection.)

Once I was in the store shopping, and I got this feeling I wanted to cry, run away. I had to leave the store to rush home to feel safe. Depression, anger, grief, guilt, and loneliness became a friend of misery from the past, conditioned by the Catholic Church. Past emotions stayed deep inside. No matter what I tried, I couldn't get rid of those feelings.

I become angry at myself thinking, *It has been a long time, let go*!

I wanted to feel my feelings in the present moment, not feelings from the past. I was living a nightmare, but I wasn't going to stop trying to live in the present. I stayed awake having busy thoughts. Did I sleep? It didn't feel like I did. My day was sometimes interrupted and the next day I might crash early in the afternoon. My sleeping disorder got so bad, I felt I didn't sleep completely, like my mind was constantly running, thinking about nothing, going back and forth. Thoughts of the past nagged me, feelings of shame and guilt, but I didn't know why. I wasn't a child any longer, and I was safe. Some of the days it was hard to function, work was extra hard, I was so tired. I couldn't figure out what was causing this. I became depressed. My family suffered if I snapped over things that weren't important. I had difficulty falling asleep and staying asleep. I just put up with the feeling of being tired all the time. But I finally had to go to the doctor. I was asked if I had any stress or was dealing with something difficult that was on my mind.

I was so surprised to see the sleep study. I suffered from sleep apnea. My sleep pattern showed that I stopped breathing throughout the night. I have to use a C-pap machine to breath at night, or I will stop breathing in my sleep,

Yes, I have too much on my mind! I believe the awful feelings were caused by my boarding school experiences. But it was even more than that. I felt an abandonment of spirit. I felt exiled and held hostage in my own country. I was unable to feel free without the equal status as other people have in my own country.

I read more and more, and tried to understand more about what affects human behavior. The National Child Traumatic Stress Network and many other sources across the fields of psychology and psychiatry highlight how minority children fare worse in the aftermath of a trauma due to the added impact of their racial inequalities.[1] They experience more feelings of being off balance, an inability to truly connect, severe depression, sense of panic, etc.

My years at Marty taught me to always be on high alert for danger, not knowing what was going to happen to me next. I kept that ongoing feeling hidden deep inside. Outside I projected a different picture and learned to live like that. I wanted to succeed, to change the stereotype of how the rest of the world sees the Indian.

But the opportunities and choices to better ourselves were in government control, giving us just enough to keep us quiet, a legacy of discrimination and genocide, isolation on reservations on the poorest pieces of land, and lost kinship with our community and culture.

The world I loved was destroyed; the other world was "the White man's way." The mental anguish and intense pain of losing everything was passed down through generations. My own history at the boarding school was part of a generational legacy of loss. So many of my relatives, both my parents, and the generation before them were in the boarding schools, but again there was not a record kept of their lives, perhaps only a name by the Catholic Church on my father's reservation and my mother's reservation. I wished there was more documentation so I

---

1. See https://www.psych.uic.edu/research/urban-youth-trauma-center/race-and-social-justice/issues-of-race-equity-and-social-justice-addressing-the-impact-of-racial-trauma-and-inequality-on-ethnic-minority-families

could find someone who survived those times. I wanted to know! (I still do.) Such information would help me move forward.

I can count the little wins I had during the many years I kept the shame and pain inside, thinking I would be judged if I showed the true me. I questioned and monitored the way I talked, the way I looked. I remained alone. I was an at-risk teen who never had a safety net to catch me. I needed and wanted to be loved; I worried about having a purpose. Dysfunctional, destructive, unhealthy relationships put me in serious jeopardy of being hurt, maybe even killed. At those times, I didn't care about what might happen to me. I had absorbed the attitude and strong message: "You're only Indian."

My self-worth, my dignity as a child who had a lot of pain, was harmed. I blamed the Catholic Church, and all those who were in charge of running the Indian Mission boarding schools, and the people who brainwashed them to abuse me. I felt I wasn't worth much of anything. I had always struggled in school. And I wasn't aware I had dyslexia until years later in my professional career when I did research for a talk and observed others who struggled with the same learning disability and comprehension. I often misspelled or wrote letters backward. I had a hard time with very simple aspects of the alphabet phonics. I had to work hard to master speaking, writing, and pronouncing every word perfectly, which was exhausting. I had to struggle to find solutions to learning. I didn't want to experience that pain of being judged.

Oddly enough, I ended up going to Presentation College in Aberdeen, South Dakota, a small private Catholic college. I was back with nuns and priests! Eventually I transferred to Dakota Wesleyan, a private Methodist university back in Mitchell where I studied social work. I was still fairly immature for a number of years, and still lacking all kinds of boundaries. Indians weren't wanted in the local towns, and we couldn't get a job. The racist attitudes toward Indians in the little South Dakota towns weren't any better than at the mission schools.

~

I was a single mother, with a son and a daughter, searching for work after college. I found my first job as a counselor in Indiana. This was an important learning opportunity for me. I had to be brave to overcome my fears working at the Indiana Job Corp, meeting young men and women from the inner cities of surrounding and other states. I was so naïve, and this was the first time since Marty that I was away from any family in South Dakota. How different it was. This was all new for me.

The first professional advice I was given by my uncle was to "be yourself, have patience, listen, and be respectful."

My mother told me to pray and ask the Creator to help me have good words to say, and it would come to me.

The other piece of professional advice I was given was on the job: "Remember to save a space, a piece for yourself, otherwise you will be eaten up by the system."

I remembered that often and still do to this day.

I had hated school so much that I never intended to work in any educational setting, but this was a trade school. The kids were a diverse group, ages sixteen to twenty-four. The goal was for the students to get their GED, learn a new trade, graduate, and move on with life. I was a counselor for two wings of female students. Let me tell you, they lived a fast life, good or bad. Some were in gangs from Chicago, Illinois, and Indianapolis and Gary, Indiana.

Early on in my job, the lead counselor followed up with me to see how things were going in my two wings of female dorms. I was about to unlock my office, which had my name written on the door, when she turned around, smiled, giggled, and said, "Look at all those gang signs by your name."

I was so embarrassed. I really hadn't known what a gang sign looked like. As I became more aware of what these kids had experienced, the violence they might have seen in their short lives, I learned things I never knew about gangs. I saw their warrior side and their having a purpose in the gang, being willing to do anything that was asked of them in the gang. That was so sad. I recognized the "mean face," just like the one I used at Marty to keep people away from me.

Many fathers of these young adults weren't part of their lives. These students had no guidance from a male figure. Their parents didn't have time to meet their needs to be nurtured, accepted, loved, or give them a feeling of belonging.

To sustain, every child needs healthy adults in their life. We all need a role model to play out what core values to follow, our values, our family values, not the values of strangers on the street or in street life. As humans we want to be connected with the people we can relate to. Wanting to be nurtured, to have purpose in life, we get our identity, allowing us to build our core value, if we belong to a community that knows who we are. If not, we will get lost looking in the mirror, not liking ourselves, feeling angry. A young person searching for a direction, wanting to change their world environment, wants a better future. They need a mentor to show them they are important. I wanted to help these young people, guide them, give them hope.

Being a young parent myself, I struggled because I didn't know how to parent. I was on my own with two children. I had to work on a tight budget and long hours. My children were practically raised by the folks who ran the preschool, then regular school. I learned mostly from books how to be a good parent, how to communicate, and how to know what is an unhealthy relationship. Remembering the abuse of my own childhood, I told myself that I would not let anything like this happen to any of my children. Their home life would be different, I will grow up and be a witness. They will not experience that kind of abuse. I would always be there to rescue them. No child should be mistreated in any form.

I tried to be a mentor to the young people I worked with, the gang members and others who I encouraged to tell me about themselves. Still sometimes after our meetings, they had a vague look of sadness or uncertainty, unclear if they made the right choice to share their feelings with me.

I saw or heard many different sides of them, and they were very respectful toward me. So many sad stories. From my own perspective of loss, I was given different points of view to see each one. After all, I was from a state where I only saw White people, and the only people of color were the Indians from local reservations. Only a small university that recruited had any Black students, and we never saw them, because they stayed close to school. I didn't have experience working with such a large body of students who lived such a different life, and whose background was dangerous and hard living in an area that was filled with gangs. It was another world from the one I came from.

Some of the young people came from broken homes. They struggled for all kinds of reasons. Some were homeless, some had a parent who gave them all the freedom they wanted to run the streets. Some had friends killed by other gang members. If they found some group that helped keep them safe, they tended to stay even if it was unhealthy. Some had their own young children who were staying with a relative. They were exposed to extreme violence and shooting at such a young age. I saw their hurt, pain, tears, lost hopes, and brokenness. It was visible on each one's face as they expressed their feelings, yet it was covered up by the street talk so no one could see the "real" them.

Many of the parents of my students were single parents, which is a huge struggle, having the role of mother and father, providing guidance and teaching about values. And so many parents can get so caught up in work, a busy lifestyle, sports, etc., and are so tired at the end of the workday, exhausted or physically drained. Parents can be so caught up working and sacrificing to provide for their children, when the simplest thing children need is love.

I couldn't promise them a better life out there, knowing the chance was slim that they'd get away from the "street" part of them. Living at the Job Corp was a safe place for many young people. And over time I became close to the students. I think of them now, and I hope they are alive and living a good life. Maybe they made a good life for themselves, and even broke the cycle of hurt and violence.

Native American Church (NAC) gathering

Church steeple

Southside of Church

St Paul Marty Indian Mission Campus

St Theresa building with student dorms, school, rec room, laundry

Cafeteria building, chapel rooms

Entrance to nuns residence

St Paul Indian Mission forefathers

Third floor dorm after 1975, drawing from author recollection

Inside the Church

Swings

Restricted playground area around old gym building

Behind Marty

Statue of Kateri Tekakwitha (Catholic Saint Catherine, Lily of the Mohawks)

Donna, age eighteen, leaving Marty to go to college

Little Girl, painting by the author

Family, painting by the author

Warrior, mixed media, by the author

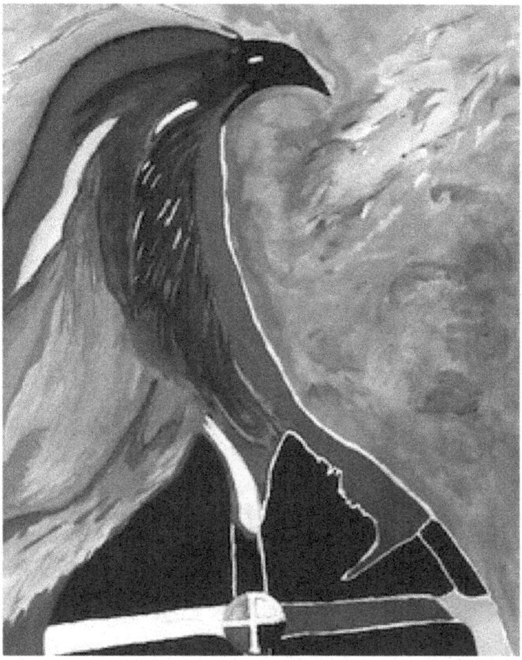

Eagle, painting by the author

Broken, mixed media, by the author

Don't see, don't speak. Mixed media by the author

Chapter 7

Promises to Young People

Catholic boarding schools committed actual crimes against children. And nothing was said openly among the Indian students. We were too scared to tell anyone about the horrific experiences we were forced to go through, plus name calling, demeaning terms thrown at us, and verbal scare tactics to control our behavior. We were all so disempowered and traumatized, ashamed and sure that no adult would believe it if we told them. I didn't know back then that we all felt that way.

But over time, Marty's reputation got around. People knew Marty was awful, that the school was abusing kids sexually, beating kids, etc. The forced manual labor was not a positive experience for any child. I never had interaction with the boys' dorms; that was forbidden; but I heard about the abuse of the boys. It wasn't talked about openly; it was a very hidden secret. For the ones who molested children, Marty was an ideal place to be. The priest and brothers did daily mass. The little altar boys spent time with the priest preparing Sunday Mass. My little sister knew a former student who committed suicide by shooting himself in the head.

I heard the rumors about the tunnel where nuns and the priest could go through a tunnel to the building to get to the children. I heard how nuns or students got pregnant by the priest, about babies who were killed or were taken away, or put in the Catholic orphanage that was run by the Church.

The orphanage is closed too, and it's sad to think about all the children who went through that place, or were put up for adoption for the White farmers for help on the farm or to help the farmer's wife. We heard of boys or girls being molested or raped. I believed this because my mother mentioned the orphanage on that one visit with her so long ago, not really saying that was the place.

If the buildings could only speak about what went on behind the locked doors—maybe we could get some justice. I never wanted to go back to that part of my life that felt so lonely. I pray for each child who was hurt or who suffered at the hands of the "righteous" people, touched by the pedophiles who prayed every day for forgiveness.

The US government was paying these boarding schools to assimilate children so they would forget being Indian; and instead they caused severe psychological and physical trauma, and a lifetime dealing with the after-effects of their abuse.

I have not yet accepted that I "survived" the school; because it is still part of my life. The after-effects calmed down some: I became a bit less angry, swallowing that lump in my throat and keeping the tears down. I haven't made peace with the harsh punishment and verbal abuse from the clergymen and the nuns.

My mother and my grandparents suffered before me in such schools. Each school had its own form of discipline. The most damaging to me was the brainwashing to believe and accept a perverted view of the Catholic religion, knowing every detail about the rituals, and being forced to adopt beliefs that were spirit-crushing, contradictory, and abusive. From generation to generation, each child was told we will never be much of anything.

I wasn't privileged. My golden-brown skin will never be white. Success of any kind was out of reach because I am Indian. The Church made me believe this. It breaks my heart to find out many privileges weren't available for me—the biggest being not to have a choice to believe in my own Creator, which I grew up with. The goal of the Catholic and other mission churches and BIA-ran and military-ran boarding schools was to destroy the people—in keeping with the government goal of genocide of the Indian people. The true history has been kept quiet for so long.

All the disappointments, depression, even all the loss in life—it was not our fault, but we were conditioned to believe that any setbacks we experienced were our own fault. I knew that I would never be equal; I know this is learned behavior. I saw the lack of equality in my parents' lives. Our family was in the late stages of survival mode, deprived of the opportunity to be self-sustaining—another goal of the government since the 1800s. I felt this injustice growing up to be poor, always having to overcompensate just to survive in a place where you feel you don't belong.

If we forget to pretend this doesn't affect us, we are only fooling ourselves. I have dealt with the feelings most of my life of how hard it was to hold onto my true Indian identity and stay positive. I see how my relatives continue to have a struggle to keep our cultural identity. I see the breakdown of the community, my elders are gone, my community is gone. I wish I could go to one of my elders now to ask what I can do to heal the trauma of the Catholic teachings.

Why did they allow us to be hit, telling me I am bad, I am going to hell? The vivid picture put into my mind the red, yellow, and orange colors of the flame I will go into. My only reassurance was that this wasn't the belief of our Indian culture.

With the breakdown of the community, where are the elders who young parents can go to? Where were the safety nets when I was growing? With so much racism, I never knew which way to go. Either way, I would be treated badly.

I decided I would mentor young people to help them to walk in both worlds. We need safety nets for our youth. With a mentor, maybe walking in both worlds won't be so hard for young people (without a church trying to control them).

~

My firstborn son was a teen and my daughter was eight when we moved back from Indiana to the Twin Cities to be near my sisters. My sister introduced me to the man who became my husband, a soldier in the US Army, with a kind heart and family who welcomed us. I learned a great deal from my husband over our thirty-plus years together.

For the next few years I worked at a Youth Diversion Program in

Minneapolis as a counselor for American Indian youth and families. Losing my own Dakota/Lakota community meant losing touch with my true Indian identity. Ripping me from my family and my culture was a terrible mistake that impacted how my four little sisters and I grew up, and affected my whole life by destroying my community and my family's way of living. Life is hard enough for an Indian who is constantly reminded growing up that we are not equal to others. So I wanted to be there for the Native youth I worked with then and throughout the rest of my working years, to help them maneuver themselves so they do not get lost, or believe they didn't have a purpose, or feel that they were thrown away.

My dearest reminder and hope as a child in pain was that nothing lasts forever, that one day I could have a good life and be proud. I prayed that someday everything would fall into place. Knowing that no one was there for me, I just wanted to be there to reach out to them, wanting to hear every word, and tell them not to be ashamed, that they have that right to have their feelings, whatever they are. So I asked my students questions. I wanted to let all of them know to be proud of who they are, that we all have a proud heritage, we must be strong and continue carrying on the banner of proudness. "Never let go of your Indianness or who you may come to be." Our history and our stories live on with our elders and the ones who went on to the spirit world. I told them, "One day you too will be a mentor to others."

When sharing my own stories and those I learned from the young adults, we laughed and cried in silence, and we learned how to embrace who we are.

I have felt very honored to have the utmost pleasure to spend time with the adults and youth who respectfully shared their stories with me then, and all through my career. I learned so much from each of them in the uniqueness of what they saw, even at a young age, the rawness of hurt they carried, and the courage they have to share, wanting to help others.

I wish that, back when I was young, someone had enjoyed my sisters and me as students just as much as I have loved my work with K-12 grades. I have always believed in my students, they have been highly intelligent and unique young people. I would not disrespect them. I encouraged them to express what is important, don't fall for or accept negative treatment.

I hoped that maybe one day, they will feel equal and deserving of having a good life. I told them, "You have the right to speak up. If you are being discriminated against, you have rights."

There are many lessons to learn in life. And my students have taught me many things: such as, one has to *earn* respect in order to *get* respect, no matter what your age. In my mind, I was enjoying my own schooling/learning along with my students. I admired each one of them.

In the Minneapolis community, I found it easy to work with Indian youth. It was good that I could see the students in our community. Most had their own problems in life. I wish I could say it was mostly growing pains, but some of them had already experienced prejudice and harsh discrimination. They already knew that Indian people are not going to experience "privilege."

I wanted all of them to keep learning the true history of our peoples. It is important not to repeat it, and to stand up for others who couldn't speak for themselves. Otherwise we will not be heard. I was teaching them to listen to what is being said, and if we don't need the advice, store it away; maybe one day, we might use that advice.

What happened in the past caused many of these young men to be caretakers for other family members, not in the traditional way like our relatives before us. The circumstances changed. They were forced to grow up at a fast pace, trying to stay positive, trying to go to school, then going home to make sure their siblings were fed and safe at home. These young men have the potential to become what they want to be. But the hard part is convincing them. That was the task I accepted at that time. But my task with these young men was difficult for me. Being an Indian woman and a mother, I struggled with my approach to teaching young men.

My father was always with us and a good provider, and we had Indian male relatives. But as a girl, I didn't have to pay attention to the male teachings. I didn't have any brothers; I grew up around all women. My mother told my sisters and me what our father had said, "These are women; you teach them."

These young men really needed a male figure in their life. This became clear one day when I had five young men as part of this group. I never had any problem with them, they were very respectful and good young men. I had to teach them to value themselves. But I think they only saw me as a mom talking to them.

In trying times, I wanted them to understand that a young Indian man is still a warrior in the world—just in different ways. So many male relatives are missing. I hope one day we will see more warriors, Indian men, out of these young men who will be fathers, role models, mentors. The future will have a men's society in the community to guide them into manhood.

I encouraged each one to not give up, mentor another young person, be a positive influence in your community. I tried to help them understand their history and try to stop the negative stereotypes about Indians. It took me a while to learn how to relate to these young Indian adolescent men without appearing to lecture or be a mom.

At a local powwow I attended, a beautiful very light-skinned Indian came up to me and took me by surprise, saying, "Your full-blooded Indian."

"Yes, I'm Dakota"

"You mean Sioux?"

I was curious, so I asked her, "Why?"

"Your skin is pretty, and you're dark. I wish I were dark. I don't like being this color. Everyone thinks I'm White."

I stopped and told her what my parents and relatives told me—that being Indian isn't about your clothes or jewelry or looks. Being Indian comes from your heart. I told her, "Don't let anyone make you feel ashamed. Be proud."

To be proud was the crux of my message to my students.

Chapter 8

Collision at Fifty-Five

One day, while I was on the way back to work at lunchtime after dropping off some food to my mother, an elderly lady ran a red light and T-boned the front end of my car. The shock of being hit hard and then being loudly screamed at by the woman who hit me triggered horrific childhood memories I thought I had hidden away. The car collision aftermath played out in slow motion as witnesses assured everyone present that the old woman was at fault. She was speeding and ran the light. Thankfully no one was hurt.

In the coming days, I felt more and more anxious as I began to take care of getting the car fixed. *If I hadn't gone out to pick up lunch, this accident wouldn't have happened.* I began to feel depressed, guilty over little things, angry over nothing, crying, feeling out of control. I stood helpless as all the memories of abuse and assaults at Marty came flooding into my consciousness.

I could only think about what happened at the boarding school, how I was shamed, punished, yelled at. I hated those feelings and couldn't figure why they came back. I remembered how the bully robbed me of my self-worth and dignity, the loneliness, how my inner voice repeated the taunting about being ugly, Black, with big lips. She wouldn't leave me alone. The violence she inflicted stayed with me.

I had told myself: *It's over, don't think about it. It's my secret. I don't have to deal with or feel those feelings again.*

No one knew all that was hidden in the deepest part of my soul, and I didn't have to tell anyone. That secret abuse was mine to keep forever. I didn't know any better; I was a child. I had no voice because

I was a poor, uneducated Indian girl. I was told I would never amount to much, and I would end up being another drunk Indian with lots of babies. Though such shaming was never part of my Indian community, I had to stay in control, not let on, not let anyone see how stressful it was to keep my secret hidden even within my own community. For all that time at Marty, perfection was my game. I was independent; oblivious to the brainwashing in the abusive school environment.

As I remained in stunned silence, I saw that sad little inner Indian child in my mind. She felt so alone, her heart beating fast, with that scared look on her face. Feeling her pain, I wanted so bad to hold her, hug her, help comfort that little Indian girl, to help her feel safe and no longer abandoned. She needed to trust and believe in me.

You can rely on me. I will not leave you behind.

Though I was now grown with a family of my own, I still had to comfort that sad little inner Indian child in my mind. Again and again, she needed to be told, "You're going to be okay. I love you."

Whenever this happens now, I give her time to gradually gain confidence, allowing her to leave this place in her nightmares behind. I want her to know she will not be staying in this horrible place, her nightmare. I reassure her that she will not be harmed or hurt; most of all, she will not be abandoned. I will make sure that little Indian girl is safe.

If she is scared or wants to cry, she holds my hand; or I just hug her to let her know that everything is okay. If she feels alone, I am there. I let her know she does matter; she is the most important person. I let her know how smart and pretty she is. I smile along with her to let her know I love her smile, and how her beautiful thick lips bring out her deep golden-brown skin. We stand tall together. There will be no more bullying or abuse.

This is hard.

You're okay, little Indian girl, just remember I am here. I know it hurts every time those memories come back.

I hold back with caution though, because if I let someone else know, I don't know if I will be safe. That awful fear returns.

What's going to happen to me if I tell?

Who will take the time to listen or make sure nothing will happen?

If I cry out, will my cries fall on deaf ears?

Who will keep me safe?

Okay, slow down, breathe, think about it. You will be okay. I'm here, look how far I brought you. So far we made it, remember? Never mind, that was scary too. Together we experienced hurtful events in our life. We overcame that big scary thing, the boogieman.

Each teacher we met along our way might have been unkind or an outright nasty human being. But we have remembered to focus on the good things, the kindness of strangers, people who have honored us just because of who you are—the many ways they've shown us how to continue to love and respect our gifts—a stranger who becomes a friend, who becomes a teacher. If you listen, you can hear their wisdom in each word they speak to our heart, our soul. Knowing that we need to slow down, be grateful, because life is what it is—our stories about where we've been or where we are in the moment.

I learned a lot in my fifty-five years of living to that point. I remembered the pain of my childhood, never really growing up, but even at fifty-five, I often felt my life had stopped because of the pain that I did not let myself feel. But I know that crisis is part of life, part of learning. Crisis is a teacher inside my soul.

My heart told me that it is time to assess my life lessons. Many memories have never been spoken or shared except in my deepest thoughts.

Now it has label, PTSD (post-traumatic stress disorder). If a crisis comes up, I *become* the crisis. Panic mode sets in.

What should I say or do? I don't know how to do this.

Then I remember the unfinished business that was tucked away, hoping I would never have to deal with that ever again. The past and the future is PTSD.

Deal with it.

I cover up my feelings, wanting to appear all put together.

It's "their problem," not mine. I have to work very hard to cover it up—until that day came when I no longer could hold it together. I wanted to give up. No longer did I want to live.

Who will listen to my cries?

I knew one thing: it was my reality. I knew I didn't want to be there. I wanted to go away. I would curl up and close my eyes. I left my body, no more scary places. I closed one door and left it closed . . .

Forever I pray.

I'm not that little golden-brown Indian girl in an Indian mission boarding school. Yes, I'm still that person; only now I'm supposed to be all grown up.

When I had a job as a school social worker, I told myself, *Yes, see I made it, I didn't have a problem, not me.*

Again I was good at fooling myself, masking my true feelings. I had a perfect world. My reality was that if I closed the door, that creepy stuff would stay away. But I couldn't ignore it. It will be part of me until I make peace or accept it for what it is.

PTSD is a teacher of the mind, like a room in our brain where we neatly put stuff away, never wanting to deal with the junk that is too painful to face.

The mistrust and letdowns as a child followed into my adulthood. The abuse controlled my environment. I was unsure how my days would go. I was unable to sleep most nights, closing my eyes, wondering when I would fall asleep. The dark is still. Closing my eyes, the darkness in my mind begins to wander. I know my reality. True to my real self, and not dealing with my childhood memories, now they are grown-up problems. I am no longer a child, but as an adult I have the same issues from previous abuse and being bullied as a child.

I needed to deal with the unfinished business of damage to my self-esteem—the impact of being treated unfairly just because I was quiet and shy. Bullies destroy a child's self-esteem. Many children who are bullied become angry, cruel adults who are unable to have healthy relationships in the community or with relatives, friends, or a spouse.

The experiences of being bullied take on a life of their own, which includes insomnia, depression, panic attacks, worry about everyone, serious health issues, and even death. A bullied child who is unable to find another person who looks or talks like them, in school or in the community, carries the traumas from their past into the rest of their life.

Internalizing and holding all the bad feelings inside, not letting anyone know what's bothering me, caused the past thoughts to get to scrambled up with the present—all because I had never processed the losses I experienced.

Every day I spent at Marty without answers, I started to believe the lie that our parents didn't love us. Seeing parents in that negative way results in a loss of respect for the people who are supposed to be the ones who keep us safe. We carried this burden into adulthood without processing the negative childhood memories.

I didn't learn the essential life skills to deal with and solve problems in a healthy way. I didn't know what healthy relationships were. Experiencing abandonment at such a young age meant becoming attached to unhealthy people in an attempt to not feel alone. Seeking happiness and connection, I sometimes entered into dysfunctional relationships and/or unhealthy work environments. Such codependency wasn't the answer. It only further harmed my self-esteem.

Having a difficult time making the right decisions, I second-guessed myself. Having been controlled in so many aspects of life, being deceived and misled (and to avoid further abuse), I couldn't be myself. I had learned at Marty how to be guarded, keep most of my feelings to myself, and not allow anyone to really know me. Even in intimate relationships, I was always afraid to be fully connected to another person, express true feelings; it kept me safe.

I kept looking for the light switch, but the room was too dark. I didn't trust anyone to tell me to turn on the light. I depended on myself only. *I'm going to find the light.*

~

St. Paul's Marty Mission Boarding School had so many fences we couldn't see: restrictions, rules, everything controlled by the Catholic Church, nuns all dressed in black. I spent time hiding, running, and living in denial. I didn't really pay conscious attention to all that while I was at Marty, but the effects of living that way came out in different ways in my adult life—I took it for granted that my mental well-being didn't need help. I wasn't paying attention to the most valuable item I have: me. Being unbalanced and denying my feelings harmed me in different ways from backaches, migraine headaches, stress, out-of-whack diabetes, eating too many carbs, causing my blood sugar to go sky high. I became my own worst enemy by trying to deny and hide from problems.

A student of mine who passed me in the hall, jokingly asked, "Why don't you say 'Hello.'"

It is difficult, takes more energy, to turn down a boiling pot.

I was trying to find balance without help for a long time. I could not afford to lose my spirituality. I depended on my community and so many of my relatives who are now gone. I grieved the loss of my uncle and auntie, who always gave me confidence and loved me. They wanted me to be successful. I no longer heard their words of encouragement: *It will work itself out.*

I thought if it might give some kind of healing or help me regain what was taken from me, I would write a letter to the bully and the nun, sister B. I remember their faces—the bully and Sister B. In my mind I saw them at the age they were when all this happened, I really didn't know what they looked like after aging, not seeing them for many years.

> *Dear Bully,*
>
> *I still can't find any forgiveness for you. Once you burn some bridges, there's no coming back. My thoughts and feelings about you run deep. I don't want vengeance, or to harm you. I only want you to know that your bullying hurt me.*
>
> *You took advantage of a young person who was so naïve. That was the first time in my life I was by myself, alone at Marty. I had no control of what was happening in my surroundings. I felt scared and helpless. The dorm nuns isolated me from my little sisters; I couldn't even see them. I will never forget this worst part of my life. And you made all those feelings even worse by making me afraid of what you were going to do to me. I was worried all the time. That was hell for me. All I wanted to do was go home.*
>
> *I blame you, Bully, and the boarding school nuns for contributing to the mental and emotional abuse that was condoned by the Catholic Church. I curse the people who inflicted the pain and traumatized me. Nothing was done about it. Where's the justice?*
>
> *Yes, you scared me. I didn't know how to react to you or to the other girls who joined in your cruelty toward me. Until you came into my life, I felt safe and sheltered from all harm from the outside world. I never before knew how it felt to be threatened. The anguish I felt*

came from your teasing, name-calling, the threats, and not knowing if and when you were going to tell the other girls to beat me up. I was jumped again and again by the girls you recruited to do your fighting. You stood to the side while they hurt me, calling me all kinds of names just to get a laugh. I don't know why you decided to pick on me. I'm not going to excuse what you did to me just because of the times or the awful place where we were living.

Do you remember how you called me "nigger lips" because of my full lips and dark skin? Your skin wasn't any lighter than mine. You had lighter hair—did that make you feel better about yourself? You were ashamed of being you—an Indian girl who wanted to be White. You couldn't change that if you wanted to.

To this day, I remember what you looked like when we were at school. I wonder if you still carry that same evil attitude, or if you ever made peace with yourself. I remember that look, the meanest smirk on your face—it made you ugly. I remember when I first saw you and the two other girls with you. You were putting your hair in a ponytail on top of your head, while you were talking to another girl. I remember her glancing at me, laughing.

You said, "It seems every time I do my hair this way, it rains. Look how light my hair and skin is." I knew you said it loud for me to hear.

The ponytail looked funny on top of your head. Did you know it looked funny? It made you look like a conehead. Your ugly smirk was like looking at me through a mirror that should have shattered. I wonder why you questioned your skin color, the color of your hair. Were you criticized for how you looked?

Bully, do you remember the day you had five girls jump me in the Rec Room, how you rubbed a pocket knife, making it hot and putting the hot blade on my arm. I wish I had grabbed you instead of the other girl. I bet she didn't know why we were fighting, because I didn't. I didn't hate her. I know her name to this day. Do you remember those names you called me, getting your gang of girls to laugh at me? Why?

I wasn't raised Catholic. I didn't understand the nuns' values, especially a nun who was a bully herself. Sister B mistreated children, hitting us, having others do her dirty work, just like you did.

I was told, "If you are being treated badly or meanly, go tell an adult." But that nun didn't believe me. That first time, I saw how the nun took up for you; she told me, "Don't be a tattletale." She never stopped you from bullying me.

I saw how a bully like you lied, denied that you bullied me, you didn't mean to hurt me, you were "only teasing." You didn't stop.

I think bullying another human was a way to esteem yourself. The control you had back then, with no one correcting you, allowed you to continue terrorizing girls smaller than you—easy prey. You took advantage, seeing how I kept to myself because I was so homesick.

Not only did you bully me, Sister B and the other nuns did too. Remember the belt line? (She is not a nun anymore; I wonder why?)

The Church was a bully, just like you. I despised the Church for making me believe the lie that I was going to hell, that I was sinner, and that people like me lived in purgatory. The Church tormented me, wanting to turn me into a Catholic so I could be "saved."

I was so afraid, I ran away. Then Sister B put me through the belt line. In order to control me, she put fear in me, criticizing me and telling me I was nothing, threatening that I will go to hell, that I was a sinner. This was how the Church used a child as an example of how you might be punished.

I know you noticed I was no longer a boarder when I went to live with my uncle and auntie. I decided I would never stay with you again on campus. I knew you were still there. After that, I noticed that you avoided me. Knowing you, you probably found another girl to make her life a living hell. When you saw me later, on the reservation, you still avoided me, leaving in a hurry. How come you didn't approach me after all we were all grown up?

Bully, at that time when I was young, I didn't realize how your words would continue to hurt me. Your bullying has haunted me for many years. Something weird can remind me of those times, it all comes back at the oddest moments. You never forget evil or the wrong done to you or to another human being. Your bullying influenced how I saw myself for many decades. Your meanness damaged an innocent soul.

I wonder, when you became a grown woman, did you ever address your nasty attitude? Are you still hateful? Did you ever stop bullying and recruiting others to do your bullying? Are you still evil and ugly, using words to put down others? Do you still neglect taking care of the emotional piece of your personal life? Was the way you were from being very unhappy yourself? Or were you just plain mean? Have you changed your callous ways in order to make true friends? Did you grow up to the knowledge that you were a mean girl? Do you like yourself now?

I'm still aware of you, and you still look like a bully to me. I see you have been a bitter person who has nothing to show for yourself. I see you now the same way I did back then—a hateful, obnoxious, and thoughtless human being who got her kicks bullying younger girls. I didn't know then how you must have felt about yourself, being resentful, insecure, raised negatively, perhaps disciplined harshly by your parents?

I know that bullies tend to feel superior, and think you have to scare others to be liked. You bullies may think you are respected, but the truth is—people just don't want to be around you.

Bully, didn't you ever have someone who respected, loved, or even thought you were a gift from the Creator? I was taught growing up that Wakan Tanka values Indian parents and children. I was treated by my parents as a gift from Wakan Tanka. That is one of the values loving Indian parents have. The Creator gave you a gift to bear children, not damage children. I cannot imagine you having children of your own.

Karma is a killer; you never know when it comes back to you. If you observe and listen, you learn how to see another person for who they are. You might have been different if you had used your skill as a leader for the good of others—you were good in rallying other girls to do your dirty work, and standing back, telling them to fight and push around girls like me. If you had been a better person, you could have been different.

One other thing, just to let you know: I was loved just the way I was when I left Marty. My Uncle and Auntie's home was full of pure love and respect for me. Their pure love encouraged me not to turn out to be a bully like you or treat anyone else as badly as you treated me. I was treated like a daughter in the Indian way; they were my parents. I had someone to protect me. I could look out for my little sisters too. I was given the Indian values to be proud of myself, show respect, and live the values I learned. They instilled these values of being Indian—to be proud of myself. I'm not that little girl you tortured. I'm more sophisticated now; I know how to take care of myself.

My Uncle and Auntie believed in getting an education, going on to college. And I did. Did you go off to college? Or did your bully attitude stop you?

Excuse me, I didn't introduce myself. I was that little girl with golden-brown skin. Do you remember your victims? Just think back and remember me as that little Indian girl you terrorized. A little history about why you are hearing these words from me: I haven't forgotten you. I didn't understand much then. I thought it couldn't get any worse from the Church or the other people who lived at Marty, my hell. To this day I can still see your mean smirk. Do you even remember hitting me, pushing me, taunting me?

Knowing you, you won't remember me or my little sisters. I really don't care whether you do or not. I am slowly letting go of how you made me so angry.

I often question myself, "Do I hate you?" All that you did to me was so horrible. But I don't know if it's really that strong an emotion as hate. Instead maybe parts of it helped me be a better person, to truly love myself. But the bullying, I won't forget; that hurt.

Bully, I did want to call you all kinds of names, kick your butt, put you down, call you the same words you called me. But I know I would not gain personally by hurting you. I was raised with the values taught in my upbringing—to respect all living beings. I'm not weak, and I won't feel powerful by bullying another person. Here is my thought for you: I am letting you know how wrong you were. I don't wish harm on you; I just want to let you know how you made my life hell as a child. But now I'm a proud Indian woman.

Donna

(And for Sister B)
Maybe God forgave you. I haven't. I remember all the punishment you poured on me. I remember the belt line, you forced me to eat tobacco and made me swallow my own puke as I was kneeling on the hard floor. I remember how you were never kind and always had that sour look on your face. I don't forgive you for the verbal or physical abuse. I never understood how or why what you did could be justified in the eyes of God, how you could be forgiven for your part in all the suffering and emotional abuse at Marty. The Church took advantage, trying to mold us, taking innocent naive children, influencing us with your hate, and destroying our dignity.

Chapter 9

Using My Voice

I ask the Waken Tankan Creator for peace. I'm only one voice, yet it is important to start speaking, even if it has taken a long time to speak out. I lost two of my sisters who I know had suffered in many ways. We all suffered losses that hindered our lives because of the abuse and the separation from our parents.

Elders like me are talking more now, maybe gaining some courage, wanting badly to heal. *What can they do to me now?* We must never forget the boarding school era. Let other public educators put the truth in the history books, and most of all let the younger Indian generations know that we must continue to stand up, fight for our right to be whole and for the government to be held accountable for the injustice.

I still seek healing, and continue to heal. I still feel shame based on certain aspects of this topic. I am still scared, questioning whether anyone is going to believe me. What matters is that it happened. I haven't forgotten that it was real; it did happen.

I do not seek a monetary compensation or gift. No money can recapture a little Indian girl's inner-spirit world or erase all the verbal attacks, shaming, victimizing, evil conditioning to feel you don't deserve anything; you're just an Indian.

The wounds deep inside, which control most of my life, cause great emotional anguish. Inside this strong woman is this little girl who feels shameful guilt and fear that she/I will be scolded and punished. When I am upset, I have to tell myself again and again, *You're an adult. This is you.*

The little voice inside was not loud enough to be heard and shout, *Look!! Look at what happened to me and all the other Indian children who have suffered emotional abuse haunts you until you die.*

This little girl was hidden deeply within me for decades. She continued to be sensitive, not daring to show true feelings, never talking about it. It was easy to cry, but over time the tears stopped. No longer a child or an adult woman, the little girl, who is part of me, didn't get that chance to heal. We were stuck in time. We had to grow up quickly, and we didn't want to take time to stop to feel, or remember trying so hard to find ways to avoid that pain.

Will I die knowing I haven't finished going through the healing process or counseling?

Those ugly memories are better off left alone.

When I finally left Marty, I promised myself I would never set foot on the grounds of Marty Mission again. It was part of the past. I really didn't know why yet, but I felt I had too. Maybe if I did, I could let go and help myself heal what happened to me and my little sisters when we were separated for the first time, and I couldn't talk to them. I could only glance at them in passing. My insides felt hollow. It was a nightmare. I couldn't sleep. I didn't know what to do.

I often wondered why I was always sad. I had a career and a wonderful husband and kids, and a second son. But something was missing. I had never talked about my time at Marty in any detail with anyone. But now I began to tell my husband a little more about it. He listened. He urged, "Tell me more."

His encouragement gave me permission to tell the truth, and feel believed.

After the scandal that hit the world news about the Catholic sexual abuse of young children, who were now adults, I had waited to hear about any Indian children who were now adults, now elders. But none were mentioned. That got me wondering. Was Marty ever punished for their crimes? The history of Marty dates back even before 1900.

The Indian Mission schools caused great harm to Indian children, and much of the true history was kept hidden. Few records were kept. Psychology and psychiatry professionals didn't learn how to counsel an Indian person who had such a veiled and traumatic history, which resulted in depression, isolation, confusion, shame, thinking the abuse was their/our fault, acting out, or covering up with unhealthy behaviors. Many who had the courage to seek help by going to counseling walked away more confused, often because the clinicians had so little to go on.

The stereotypical view of a private boarding school is where a child can get a good education then go off to an elite college. The parents of such students were often well off. This was far from the case with Indian mission boarding schools. The truth about the corporal punishment, sexual abuse, and physical and emotional abuse by the Catholic Church in South Dakota and in other states with indigenous populations, which damaged Indian children in the sixties, continued to fall to deaf ears—or on those who felt, "They're only Indian."

Remembering all this, I had so many questions that my head was spinning. I was angry! I wanted answers. Why weren't Indian boarding schools mentioned in the news—why weren't we good enough to have justice? Indian children were abused physically, emotionally, sexually, and verbally.

So if I say something, what will happen? Nothing, it happened so long ago, who would remember? I wish it was that easy to forget it—the horror is frozen in my memories. Will the administrators and promoters of the Indian boarding schools where these horrific crimes against Indian children occurred ever be held responsible, be punished, and account for all their damage to young Indian children who are never able to heal? This harm hindered their mental, social-emotional growth and development, and created chaos in their young minds.

I decided to carry out my own research to learn more. I wanted to close that chapter of my life. I wanted my mind to dump that garbage of the past and put my life in a better place. Any information would be welcome. To this day I don't know the real reasons this happened to me and to so many others. The reasons are still hidden. But Marty mission school did exist, and I wanted some answers. I wanted to see the truth in black-and-white print instead of the fog of my memory.

Knowing some answers wouldn't change the abuse, cruel treatment, and disrespect that children endured, I still wanted my records from the schools I attended, to see the dates, and the reasons I was sent to Marty. All institutions had to keep records, right? Especially those that accepted money from the government for each Indian child sent there.

I wasn't only interested in the years. I wanted to know what was real. I wanted to know if I was important enough to be counted as one of those students of any background. I wanted to see my name, grades, a progress report, anything to give me a clue—some evidence that I and my little sisters existed.

I contacted my elementary school in Mitchell, knowing they had to keep records. I wrote, giving my permission to release my school records, then I called, asking if they found my records. They said no, they had transferred my school records to Marty back in the sixties.

I couldn't find any recorded information regarding our being taken from our parents and placed at Marty. I asked the tribe if my school records were directed to the new Marty school. I contacted the tribe, telling them the school said they had transferred my records to Marty Mission Indian Boarding School. But nobody had the records. The Catholic Church didn't have them, the tribe of the New Marty Indian School didn't have them, *so who does?*

What happened to my school records, the records of an Indian child?

I went in person to ask to see records. But I was told they no longer have records about our time at Marty. When the boarding school was closed, without admitting any ownership of the abuse and harsh treatment that went on there, they gave all "paperwork" to the tribe, but there were no records to see. Where did the records go? Wasn't child abuse reported back then? Was it legal to mistreat children? A child back then had no rights.

Student boarders were the only ones to attend church daily along with the nuns at Marty. I never saw anyone else at church except us—no townspeople or other witnesses to the treatment of the children at Marty. Without records, there was no evidence of abuse and the higher officials of the Church could transfer the bishop elsewhere, maybe even to another country, and the Catholic Church could avoid a scandal, and hope everyone would forget what happened.

Indians in general didn't have any rights in those days anyway; discrimination was accepted at large by the White community. But there were witnesses to the abuse. We all saw others berated and physically harmed, emotionally manipulated and mistreated. Many students were well aware of the sexual abuse that happened to other students.

I am still here, still scared, knowing it was true. Even as an adult, I felt I didn't have the right to ask for or deserve answers, or to be provided with the truth, the real history. *Who will I offend if I correct the misinformation about my history?*

The emotional pain is hidden, but the abuse we went through is real. Indian people have gone through a harsh history, not being considered human, so much so that we didn't consider *ourselves* to be human. *Where do we belong?* I suffered anxiety, depression, criticism, sleep disorder, unhealthy relationships, manipulation by others, making bad decisions, bad choices. I lost a sister who was at Marty with me. She passed away, still damaged by the emotional abuse, carrying all the pain with her to the spirit world.

Knowing all that happened to me, I sought answers, but I could never find paperwork or a person to help me find any. No former students were willing to share their personal experiences or their feelings about nuns, priests, or what they knew about the abuse during their time at the school.

Most were so uncomfortable, they would only say, "It was strict and some of the nuns were mean." Some said they didn't mind being there, because it was better than being at home.

When talking with one of the nuns, she told me that the tribe did have all the school records. But no one knows where the records are. I questioned whether there was a file on me with notes written regarding my grades, my adjustment at school, progress reports, or if they ever notified my parents that I ran away, whether they were concerned about how long I was gone, was anyone contacted, was someone sent looking for me, what kind of discipline punishment did I receive by the dorm nun, Sister B? How about something about how I was bullied severely and physically, verbally, and emotionally abused, and how that affected me? Was it documented how I was slapped backhanded, leaving a hand print on my cheek by priest Father Cashmere, or had to walk the belt line and made to eat my own throw up?

I had so many questions about what was done to me. But nothing was recorded anywhere. No one was even aware of how I was treated or what happened to me. Nothing was done.

In 1975 Congress passed the Indian Self-Determination Act, giving most boarding schools back to the tribes. With no financial assistance, the Church picked up and left. Legally we can't hold the Church liable to make their wrongs right.

No more money would be given by the government, and the Church couldn't afford to house these little Indian children.

Marty didn't close because of the abuse or a sex scandal. It closed because the bucks stopped coming. No responsibility was taken by the Church, which moved on to another "holy" assignment.

I haven't heard of a plan offered to help healing the damage they caused to so many.

Chapter 10

Generational Trauma

I lived the best way I knew how, yet the life I was living always felt like I was doing everything wrong. I didn't feel normal. The world and people around me appeared to be normal, that they "got it." I thought, *I'm educated now, so how come I didn't get it?*

I lived in denial most of the time, allowing myself to learn most things the hard way. It was so hard to explain why I was hurting. I stopped myself from feeling my true emotions. I was unable to find a professional who could help or even begin to understand the Indian Mission School or BIA that we were made to attend.

Get over it! I am an adult, not a little girl who went numb and was able to leave her body to stop the pain.

Hiding, running, being in denial, I wasn't paying attention. But what I was feeling deep down came out in the form of backaches, migraines, stress, and diabetes that caused more problems on the outside. I looked like I was taking care of myself. It was not easy to tell myself the pain would go away. I took my mental health and well-being for granted, and I could no longer depend on my community of relatives. They were gone. I had lost the two who always gave me confidence—Uncle and Auntie. I just wanted to hear their words again: "Not to worry; it will work itself out."

All the money I spent on therapy and self-help books didn't work or provide me with any comforting thoughts. None of it addressed the abuse at the Indian mission boarding schools. I believe in therapy and working out issues with a therapist, but I couldn't find a therapist who knew about the Indian boarding school history and resulting trauma.

I made promises that I would do something so children will not be treated horribly. It was hard to admit, to have the courage to name "trauma" for what it was. I walked slowly, took extra time to process hate, had to be on high alert and careful, remaining a very private person, not trusting. I did not allow anyone to get close to me. I was comfortable allowing only a very few friendships. My true friends were my sisters who were at Marty, "the Marty five." Only they knew what it was like at the boarding school. I didn't trust many people or want to share my shameful story of my boarding school days. It was the hardest thing to say out loud.

I didn't want to recreate chaos from the past. I didn't want to overthink something small. I became disorganized easily, anxiety set in, at times it spiraled out of control if I made a mistake, being conditioned to obey all rules.

I shouldn't be still hurting, right? Am I crazy? Am I the only one who carried these kinds of hurt for such a long time? To this day, I don't have the answers.

If someone else told me the same story as what I experienced, I would think, *It was so long ago. Why is it so important to struggle all these years with your feelings?*

My sisters and I had to learn to deal with the pain in our own ways. I did a lot of reading of self-help books dealing with emotions and tried to apply them to what I was feeling. I tried to put a name on something that was bad in our childhood.

In order to begin the healing process, I had to look at the big picture, the history, the reason they built this type of school and took these Indian children away. I had to name the wrong that was done. I needed help in sorting out where the emotions belonged.

~

The Bureau of Indian Affairs (BIA) established the first Indian boarding school in Washington State on the Yakima Indian Reservation in 1860 as part of a so-called "well-intentioned" long-term plan by reformers, Herbert Welsh and Henry Pancoast, to "civilize" Indian people and assimilate them into the American mainstream beliefs and values. However, assimilationists were eventually not satisfied that Indian children were "sufficiently removed" from the influences of their tribal lives. The solution was to create off-reservation boarding schools.

When the US Congress first provided funds for education and the civilization of Indians back in 1819, creating the first Christian schools for Indians, the schools were run by the White churches and the (also White) federal government. The "civilization" of Native people came without the same privileges that White people took for granted.

Institutional racism influenced the laws used to regulate Indian nations (who had no rights, no votes). The White powers in control in government, churches, schools, and business called us pagans who didn't believe in God (or say God's name the same way they did).

In 1879 Colonel Richard Henry Pratt established the first off-reservation boarding school for American Indians in Carlisle, Pennsylvania, and served as its headmaster. His motto was, "Kill the Indian, save the man," and he launched an all-out assault on Native cultural identity.

Students at Carlisle, and eventually at all other Indian boarding schools, were not allowed to speak, even to each other, in their own native languages. Corporal punishment was standard. Such boarding schools emphasized agriculture, industry, and domestic arts with minimal academic subjects. Conversion to Christianity was part of the curriculum. Severe discipline, confinement, diet restriction, and disease epidemics (measles, TB, etc.) occurred regularly in these boarding schools.

Many Indian families across the country refused to send their kids to these boarding schools, and Indian agents withheld rations or used police threats to get families to cooperate. In 1893 mandatory education for Indian children became law. To enforce the federal regulation, Col. Pratt took Apache prisoners to Augustine, Florida, rapidly removing the Indian children from their culture and subjecting them to strict discipline and hard work to force them to assimilate into mainstream society. A similar model spread to other schools.

Benedictine priest, Father Sylvester Eisenman, came to Yankton, South Dakota, as a missionary in 1918, to "help Sioux Indians." He began by taking fuel, food, and clothing to Indian homes and giving communion and baptizing the adults and children to become Catholic. He learned the Native language and said it was helpful in reaching more converts to Catholicism to speak to Indians in their own language. He helped gain funding for the St. Paul Mission in Marty on the Yankton Reservation.

Father Sylvester felt that the Native American Church wasn't going to save the Indian people, that NAC was "devil's work," and the Indian boarding schools would be more successful if they were Catholic—and Catholicism was the only religion to be practiced. In 1922, he became the head of St. Paul's Indian Mission Boarding School at Marty. The Father became a lucrative fundraiser for Marty Mission, sending letters across the country for people to help his "little ones." It was easy to solicit donations from the wealthy by describing how these poor, ignorant children needed to be civilized. The Marty boarding school was built with donated money and labor. The Father also had an orphanage (Placid) for unwanted Indian babies. When the children reached kindergarten age, they were placed in the Marty boarding school.

Throughout this time, Indians across the US were not given a choice to practice our ceremonies, almost everything about being Indian was forbidden, like concentration-camp confinement, yet without fences. Times were extremely harsh, and Native families had to depend on the BIA government rations.

It was all too easy for the Catholic Church to manipulate Indians into becoming Christian, taking all our children and placing them in institutions. There was no law to protect our children. Marty and the other Indian boarding schools run by the Catholic Church were basically institutions to house Indian children until they are able to leave as adults or run away. If runaways were caught, they were harshly punished and beaten. These types of injustice were not new; many adult Indians were placed in asylums even if they were not mentally ill. White people didn't know what to do with any Indian person.

Catholicism in the 1930s still had control over Indian children. Many of the Church's clergy had been White settlers with no respect for or interest in understanding Indian culture, fearing the so-called Godless savages. Needing land for farming, settlers saw Indians as in their way.

Native people in the US have suffered a long history of being misrepresented and treated unjustly in order to meet the goals of so-called "assimilation," which is more correct to term as "genocidal annihilation"—intentional actions to destroy and erase a specific group of people. Native people are the victims of historical generational trauma, which we all need to admit out loud, and not feel ashamed to feel. Give it a name.

I have the right to name it and to tell my story. Physical, sexual, and emotional abuse of a child causes the same type of trauma that results in outcomes such as anger-turned-inward, self-medication, post-traumatic stress disorder (PTSD), dysfunctional behaviors later in life, self-harm, and more. Indian families have been given no resources to address the trauma of their history or the traumas associated with genocidal annihilation.

Unspoken hate feelings have nowhere to put the blame. A child learns early to pack away those feelings (just like Marty Mission school taught us) and maintain a disconnection from ourselves and from feeling the sad, hurtful emotions, while sliding into depression, wanting to self-harm, wanting not to feel, doubting one's own being.

Suicide wasn't even reported among Indian people; no mental health resources existed. The wider attitude was that Indian people brought this all on themselves by being dependent on government handouts. Taking the land and placing all Indian people on reservations to depend on the government for everything (which was not much) was not our doing, not our choice. The reservation was and is poor, offering nothing. The hardship and lack of basic healthcare has caused many deaths.

To know that our own race was so hated is a painful experience for the Indian. Genocidal murder of a culture, tearing apart families, and the placement of children in educational institutions; severing the parent-child bonds, leaving Indian people with no legal, social, or ethical justice, and destroying their future—all over a piece land and the mineral gold—was brought on by the simple greed of White people in the United States.

Many Indian men served in the US armed forces even before Indians were recognized as citizens in 1924. We could fight but we weren't good enough to have the legal right to protect our culture, language, religion, or choose how we will be educated. And becoming a citizen didn't guarantee that any Indian would be treated well or fairly.

The hardships of Indians were no fault of those who were denied the privileges enjoyed by White families. Starting in 1758, when the US government first took Indians off the land and placed them on isolated and fairly useless tracts of reservation land, Indians could no longer live off the land.

When Indians were able to move freely, live anywhere, and stay as long as they wished on the open land the creator gave us, we had what we needed. But we were put on worthless pieces of land, and told that this was our permanent home.

Indian people were natural farmers who lived in interactive communities that together grew what was needed for food and created medicines from herbs in the forest. We had our own government. We had our own societies to run the tribes. We had elders who counseled the people. Our culture was conditioned to help each other, appreciate what we have, and not waste.

My mother's mom knew the stress Indians felt living on a reservation with restricted boundaries, having to live in an assigned area with an invisible fence to keep the Indians in one place. Indian people had poor healthcare and hospitals, not enough housing, and the conditions in the housing that existed were poor.

In the beginning, the government housing probably looked nice, but every original appliance and countertop was worn out, not fixed when broken, and the housing was no longer worth living in. Indian people are not lazy and don't want to live below the poverty line, but they have no job opportunities, and few positions to fill.

The government created the hardship for Indian people to depend on unhealthy monthly rations handed out, which created unhealthy, high-carb diets that caused diabetes and other health problems.

The reservation was no safe haven for the parents whose children were systemically taken away from their families and placed in the BIA, government-funded, mission schools. Parents' lives were now idle and in greater isolation. The reservations left Indians without opportunity, and everyone lived in poverty.

The government had placed reservations far from major towns or cities, far from hospitals, schools, stores, and essential businesses. The government determined who could get a bank, grocery store, local school, good gas station. Same with decent healthcare. The discriminatory practice of redlining was in full force—a systemic denial of services to non-Whites. With limited financial resources, no start-up money, no loans, no collateral, Indians were separated from surrounding businesses off the reservation. White people in neighboring towns had banks, thriving businesses, and other necessities. But Indians couldn't have our own banks or our own businesses. Any business on the reservation was run by White people.

Even grocery shopping in the neighboring towns was a form of redlining. Finding the essentials around the reservation was not easy or affordable. Going miles away is a hardship requiring a vehicle and gas just to get food. The overall discrimination made it difficult for anyone from the reservation to become successful. Indians were treated as "less than." Hopes and dreams were out of reach with limited resources, and too often ultimately crushed.

For any person who has not experienced this type of systemic racism, it would be hard to understand what it feels like not to have that one thing—privilege—that makes all the difference.

Discrimination kept people on the reservation. The local towns were not welcoming, and people there would prevent Indians from having many resources that might be available. Indians heard, "You don't qualify, you are not eligible." We could not have the same equality and advantages and benefits as the White community.

Even now, if I wanted to go back and build a home on the reservation land, I couldn't go to the bank and get a large loan to complete the home. Building a home requires more than the structure; I'd have to pay a high cost to buy pipe for running water, electrical lines, and other materials and building supplies and transport them back to the reservation. If you are able to build on your own, you need collateral for a loan, which can't be the land since you inherit it. The government controls whatever can and cannot be built on the reservation.

The entire arrangement is set up to keep Indians dependent on the government.

In her book, *A Framework for Understanding Poverty*, Ruby K. Payne, PhD, described how generational poverty is passed down from one generation to the next, who are then limited in the support systems and resources needed to survive financially, emotionally, mentally, and spiritually. In the hidden rules of the middle class, Indians had no financial resources to take advantage of. How they were treated by the government and society left them with no recourse for obtaining emotional help, especially for the breadwinner who could not get a job.

The government plan kept Indians poor, stuck, and giving up what little hope we might have, no longer even able to depend on our Indian community, all of whom were suffering too. The rule of "the haves and have nots" in the White man's laws has been hard to understand for Indians who do not see the loopholes that made it so easy to take back what was written on legal piece of paper, a treaty. Our role models were destroyed by the broken treaty agreements and the breaking up of Indians' family systems, taking away the children, trying to make them into something other than an accepted member of a proud Indian community. We were not even considered citizens in our own country until 1924.

It makes a young Indian person angry, learning the history of how our families were separated and how we weren't included in the history books, and then the shock to learn the truth after being told lies for so long—as I was taught in the White elementary school—about Christopher Columbus, celebrating that one day, then dressing up like Indians on Thanksgiving, making paper headbands and paper feathers, making whooping noises, and being told how the Pilgrims fed the Indians; singing the "Ten Little Indians" song, then pledging allegiance to the American flag.

White kids who were and are so cruel were not born racist or prejudiced; this was learned behavior, a form of ignorance that is still passed from generation to generation. They repeated what they learned from home. The world has ignored the truth of our history, and the truth about the way Indians have been treated, and the truth we can see and feel in our lives every day—that it is twice as hard to find a job, or a decent home, or to live freely without being afraid. Discrimination is a lifetime lesson we cannot forget.

Even if we were to become fully "assimilated," speak English perfectly, and dress like the White community, we still cannot pass "Go."

We are still Indian.

Over and over what was promised to help the Indian people on and off the reservation was not delivered. Indian people are still in dying need of healthcare, mental health care, housing, and relevant education. These are not new issues; I have heard this over and over and wonder *will it ever get done*? Indian people are very aware, those issues will be pushed back with each new administrator who takes office, we don't have any political power; the pushback will come once again. Indian people have had many promises broken.

I often heard my mother say she was supposed to get forty acres along with a mule to plow a piece of land she really couldn't do anything with. She said she was still waiting for forty acres, a mule, and a plow. One time when money was promised to many Indian tribe members, she said, "I won't see it in my lifetime, or even after I die."

I am thankful to the Creator for the children who didn't listen when they were told to allow the Indian within to die. I would have thought that declaring war against children would be enough to open the ears and eyes and minds of all Americans that this was a bad idea, but sadly it was not. Americans remember much of what they did to Black slaves and are sorry. Americans remember what happened to the Jews in Europe, and have said, "Never again." But Americans in general refused for centuries to acknowledge what was done to Native people, wanting to forget the lies, the slaughter, harsh punishments, and the sexual abuse that was meant to force the devil out of the Native American children who were beaten when they cried from homesickness. Those who attempted to run away were chained and put in makeshift jails in an attic or closet for punishment. All types of acts of abuse were committed upon Native American children, carried out to accomplish the US objective to destroy Native Americans and their culture.

Nothing can tame the anger I feel for those losses.

~

Some of what I miss most was my parents having conversations in our language and how they laughed so happily. I really felt good having our home warm and safe and feeling loved by my parents. In a conversation I would hear half-Dakota, half-English. But then one day we only heard English words. We were required to speak English. Our own language was forbidden; we had to be "assimilated." Over time, our language was being lost as my people were forced to give up what made us Indian people.

The first words that were spoken to me were Dakota/Lakota. Having both parents fluent in our original language, I had no problem understanding what was being asked or said. I often wondered when my mother or father looked puzzled while having to do any kind of business with the English language. Though we were made to learn and only speak English, no one helped translate for us.

We didn't fully understand the White man's language. In those days the English speakers frowned and made fun of us, shamed us, and told us we couldn't speak our language.

Indians my age/generation spoke more English than any Indian language. My mother often said she missed talking. She said, "I'm forgetting some words I was taught as a child."

When asking her how to say a certain word, she had to think a bit longer to say it.

I encouraged my children to learn our language, to know some of the words. I hoped they would speak both. I talked with my youngest son in Dakota to let him learn more words. His grandma took care of him when I was working, and I knew my mother would speak Indian to him. It is the birthright for all young people to know their language, what tribe they are from. One of my greatest losses was that I couldn't speak my language openly. I feel jealous when I hear other nationalities speak their native tongue. Why were they allowed openly to speak and keep their language and religion, but Indians were not? We were cheated, and now we struggle to recapture who we once were.

I know my tribe: Lakota/Dakota/Nakota. I am enrolled and carry a card stating my blood degree. My blood count is thin. My full father was enrolled in a different tribe from my mother's tribe, automatically cutting my "Indian blood."

The US government gives each Native American an enrollment number to identify by "how much Indian" we are. To this day, we are the only ethnic group in the US to be registered by the government in this way. It's not a number tattooed on our forearm like the Jews under Hitler in Nazi Germany. Instead, we Indian people carry a card for life—until each generation of our tribe's blood is thinned out to nonexistence, which is the goal of genocide.

"I have my red blood card," I say jokingly about my Certificate Degree of Indian Blood (CDIB). Yet it has me troubled: why it is only Indian people have to prove they are Indian? The "blood quantum" laws created by the US government to define racial populations groups make it very difficult to get enrolled in one's home tribe. That seems to be the point—to limit entitlements to property or benefits. I was told or explained how this works, and I found it very confusing to understand. Seems to me like another form of genocide, cleansing of the Indian race to get back the land or whatever was promised in the treaties. Even if a person is a full Indian, our blood is cut by different tribes. Since my father came from Pine Ridge, my mother from Yankton, two different tribes, the blood was "thinned out."

My children's children will not qualify to be enrolled at all.

I have adjusted to the worldview of a society that doesn't typically say out loud that I don't belong here anymore. Europeans came to America often because of their own religious persecution, wanting to have their own beliefs, and also wanting the land that Indians occupied. Language (and the ability to understand the subtleties of an unfamiliar language) were used against many Indians in negotiations to take the land. Promises made were never honored. Over time (1877 to 2020) the recorded facts have changed in history books. Native people may have some protections now, but throughout most US history, Indians were the victims of hate crime.

Most of my life as a young Indian girl, I wasn't allowed to dream. I had nothing to look forward to. I learned that anything and anyone can disappear or be taken from you. I knew at an early age that I would never have the privilege, or be accepted, or have the same social status that White people have. I wasn't lazy or abnormal; I was treated that way simply because I was "only" an Indian, less than. If I saw an Indian admired or accepted, it was as a performer: a tourist might say, "Look Mommy, there's an Indian!" Otherwise the town people didn't want to be near us. We were discarded, looked upon with disgust.

Native people are still among the poorest in America, segregated in reservations into one big box of nothing. And those who left the reservations don't want to go back. Sadly there's nothing to be offered there, and the community sees those who left as "different" and no longer welcome anyway.

I remember how over time, things changed for my father. Slowly he gave up, became depressed. Racism caused unequal barriers that kept him from making a living for his family. Self-anguish was killing him slowly. His dream was to raise us off the reservation so we might have a chance for a good living. Our community was dying slowly by then, people were questioning their survival. The men in the community were suffering just as much as my father. How can you believe if you are losing hope within yourself?

He struggled, though it wasn't his fault. White society told him he wasn't good enough. Looking back, my father was depressed to have lost his community. He never wanted to be pitied, he wasn't raised that way. He was a proud Teton Oglala man—not the labels that came from the White community.

All Indian men are important. I have seen many young men struggle with what role they fit in. Each generation's trauma was passed down to the next generation of men. Uncles, sons, and grandsons were losing their role models. My father lost his father, his role model, when he was young, due to sickness. Very few elders were left, most were gone.

Indian men were put in an environment that was a set up to fail. Indian men endured, but were unable to grieve so much loss of the life that was taken from them. They could never experience the privilege of being able to give back, to raise their sons to be proud men.

Most important was their loss of being a man, failing to learn and teach how to be a father to their sons, and in the process they will lose their future sons. Blaming themselves, medicating their loss and grief with alcohol, drugs. Poor healthcare, not trusting the hospital, they died young, killed by treatable diseases. So many of our Indian relatives died from complications of diabetes, just as my mother did in 2010.

The young boys I went to boarding school with are gone, many dying young rather than living in a world that wasn't ours, where they could never fit in. They could never be a White man, or speak or look like one. Stories of the elders who had once attended these schools were never shared because of their fear and shame. Without positive things in life, they experienced hardship. Some took their own life, or lived with the pain about what happened to them, ending their lives in car wrecks, or using alcohol to self-medicate. Just like the girls, they too had many losses. They were cheated, robbed of their manhood.

Why remember something that was so horrible? What good could come from it?

I live with the psychological effects of ignorance of our collective history and connections, of White supremacy, of a government perpetrated campaign to dehumanize Indian people. My narrative bears witness and provides a personal account of those who walked on this earth; to provide a personal testament, to the effects of and truth about American History so reconciliation and healing can begin.

My community wasn't given a chance to heal, or have counseling to deal with the great losses we had. How do you comfort a community if the truth isn't told about how we got here in the first place? This has to change. Admit it in the history books. No more stereotyping. Look at the reservation, look at housing, look at the surroundings where Indian people were placed. Indian people never lived this way before, never chose this way of life. Poverty was handed to Indian nations; we were an experiment in genocidal, systematic killing of a culture.

We should not be judged by how much Indian blood we have, or by the color of our skin, or whether we "look" Indian.

Many Indian elders carry their pain deeply hidden inside. What apology will give peace? What kind of justice can be rendered to all the parents back then whose children were taken away? Admit it was wrong—everything that was done to parents and children, the many lies told to Indian families, the assumption that it was okay to destroy our dignity.

The reservation is the poorest place in America. The people who live there (and have the right to live there) need resources to build their own businesses instead of fighting for funds; they need Indian-run schools to attract Indian educators; they need decent housing (The HUD-built homes are falling apart and there is not enough money for their upkeep; they need mental health resources so our youth are not killing themselves or dying from drug overdoses, feeling they don't have a purpose. They say we are a "sovereign nation," but we are still poor.

Native parents living on the reservation had a similar childhood. No resources, no training, no business classes offered to the community. We must mentor individuals who want to build, give back, and support the community. Don't fault the people. The government still has the "say so" on Indian land and funding that still relies on blood count; the head count of how many members are enrolled in the tribe. Redlining is alive and visible on my reservation. Politics that still play a big role in Indian life.

The hardships of my parents, and the unbalance, unfairness, and racism that my parents, sisters, and I suffered and witnessed when I was a child are still alive and in place on the reservation.

I will not forget or be told to get over it. It happened for such a long time. Time does pass, but a child who was abused and mistreated will always carry that pain. Everyone handles it differently. Some turn out okay; others don't. I will always pray for all the Indian children who died in the boarding schools. I can never forgive the Catholic Church because of their philosophy of torture and brainwashing of so many children who were made to attend these types of schools. The nuns were not motherly or innocent. They never paid for their sins or their crimes of abuse, which were seldom reported. How did the Church have their sins forgiven with no punishment, only hiding their sins, transferring perpetrators elsewhere to unexpecting children, to be repeated with other children?

I see many Indian graves with no dates on them, only their tribes to let the parents know. I'm sure there are many things we still don't know about what happened to those children. We don't have the resources to honor those children who were loved and cared about, and who were a gift of their Creator.

The Native American Church (NAC) continues to keep many of the old ways. Men perform many of the roles in Indian ceremonies, and we're losing more of those elders. Many men have died. With our elders gone, any fluent speaker can pray in our Indian language. The faces change, and it's good to see many young people trying to keep the Church going strong. The prayers are like songs to the Creator. To understand every word when I was a child, and hear the synchronizing of the drum and the gourd, and the harmonized singing flowing all together was so beautiful. I hope that one day, our language will come back as we teach and share the true history of our people. I hope that our young people will continue to learn about our Native beliefs and share their Native languages. We need more people to take on the role to maintain the ceremonies and uphold the traditions, but this is harder to come by as each generation is growing up in different times.

I see the Native young adults I have been working with throughout my career as the strongest advocates for justice, wanting their true history to be taught. I will not lose hope. I will continue to encourage the young to be proud of their Indianness.

Chapter 11

Empowering Indian Youth

When I first worked with native students in a public school in St Paul, Minnesota, they made a connection to me because I am an American Indian. I found that even the smallest bit of information I taught them about their culture made them want more. I knew it was important to share with students the real history of what has happened to Indian people. I took that opportunity to teach those interested and willing to listen, making sure the students knew the truth about our brutal past, the dissolution of tribal government, the creation of reservations, having no equal representation in government, the breakup of Native families starting in the 1800s, and the many other painful things some human beings were willing to do to others for financial gain and to strip Native peoples from their true identities under the guise of "civilizing" us and "assimilating" us into the mainstream of American culture.

Young people had not heard their relatives talk about these things—too painful a subject, a lot easier to keep quiet.

The students learned about how moving forward with a strong self-image was difficult for their forebears, how education meant brutal mistreatment of children, and efforts to keep them (us) from knowing that we come from proud people with a rich cultural heritage, and finally how the US Congress only passed the Indian Child Welfare Act in 1978, which brought an end to the federal government policy of forcing Native children into boarding schools.

The students easily understood how the practice appeared to be perfectly designed to destroy what it meant to be Indian, to destroy our sense of belonging and identity, and how many Native people were unable to leave the reservations because they were not sure of themselves, not sure how they could survive the barriers to jobs and housing in the outside world.

My students could not fully understand what it meant for Indian people in those early days who never had equal rights, let alone understand the spoken words of the English language, how they were ostracized, expelled from their own homeland, placed in a desolate bare land with no shelter and nothing, and left to starve or fall victim to the diseases that killed most Indian tribes—another form of the genocide and a systematic killing of our culture. The students who shared their thoughts were sure that they would never let such things happen to them. They asked why their ancestors couldn't do anything about the unfairness. Some struggled with their self-identity, asking, "Where do I belong?"

With greater understanding, many students were angry, yet eager to learn more, and they wanted to make a difference within their school, and bring awareness in their community. They became mentors to younger students in elementary schools. They wrote to schools and obtained permission to go one day each week to talk to young Native children. I was and still am so proud of so many students who did and are doing great things to support their own communities, advocate for themselves, and bring awareness and education to their peers and others.

One student wrote a research paper as a project for class, "The reasons why Indian children were taken away and sent to a boarding school by the government was to break up the family." The student wrote about the Indian children who were harmed by the government taking land from the Indian people even though it was promised to the people, and agreed to, and they signed government treaties. He wrote, "In 1869 the government required Indian agents to hire personnel for the reservation in the relatively short time. It was decided that the reservation schools were not very successful because Indian children were too close to their homes and family culture. After almost 400 years of oppression, and no end to the brutality of the White settlers toward Indians, the reservation boarding schools were a new way to shrink and destroy Native culture. They were coming for the children—to destroy us in the Indian wars against children."

~

Building trust with young Native male students was not always as easy for me as with the female students. Many Native boys came from an unhealthy background, but no one would tell me that. No matter how bad it gets where they live, such students don't tell the family secrets. Many didn't have a father or male role model in their home or in their community to help them see how to be a man and how to interact with others as a man. The nuclear family had been all but destroyed.

One such tenth grader shared with me that he wanted to be successful, get a job, not be poor, most of all not be homeless, and was to that point tired of living with grandma, aunts, or friends. Going back to live with Mom would not be all that good or safe—putting up with people coming and going at all hours at night, getting drunk or high most of the time. This had begun to effect school. To live in a shelter would call too much attention to their living situation. So this student was staying at a friend's place on the floor or couch. He had no choices.

We all need to hear their stories and end the secrets, so their healing can begin. We all want the same things in life, to find our place in the world, where we really fit in. Every young Native student I knew wanted to fit in, find a place within an environment that didn't look like them or even recognize them as Native American. I saw and heard their disappointment when they were told they didn't "look" Indian. Most knew their tribe, had been part of a ceremony, or a pow-wow in the summer months. At another local high school where most of the students were White, and all the teachers were White, the few Native students I met were very studious and well-mannered. One boy was very traditional; he had learned singing on the drum from his father. Often when I visited such schools, Native students told me that "most of the teachers and students don't even know I am Indian," naming their tribe with great pride and a sense of honor.

In a conversation with students wanting to have an Indian name, they asked, "How is that done? Who does it?" The school's philosophy was that everybody has the same identity—but that didn't include American Indians' identity. Identity was important to my students. They wanted to know their tribes' culture and tradition, not how others saw them. Sadly, some felt they were stereotyped based on how they were supposed to look, or how dark or light their skin was.

Many Native young people won't have enough of their own tribe's blood to even qualify to be Indian, and having the right to say they are Indian is an important part of their cultural identity. So they suffer from the injustice of not "belonging." True stories about this are important to remember and put in history books. Many of my students put a great deal of effort into researching a relative and their tribe, but were faced with the added injustice of having to prove their actual Indian blood. They were often still turned down by the BIA and not recognized if some of their relatives came from a different tribe.

Students complained that the subject of Native American history was skimmed over quickly and lightly in their schools. I figured the teachers were probably afraid to tell the true history of American Indians all over the United States—if they knew it. However, I have found some teachers who are invested in the truth and will go the extra mile to teach more about it and create projects on the subject.

Some sample comments from students:

Grade 12. "I am Ojibwe, It is important to have Indian education, so I can learn about my background. They can teach me about truth, humility, honesty, courage, respect, love, and wisdom."

Grade 11. "I am a Lakota Sioux. I am more than frybread. I am more than pow-wows. I am more than alcohol abuse. I am a learner of two different cultures. I'm an academic achiever. I am an athlete, a teacher, and a learner. I will give back to my Native community. I will not be just another statistic. I will graduate college, and I will get back what was taken. I am very powerful."

Grade 9. "I am more than a woman in the United States. I'm a woman fighting to get back the respect for Native Americans. School today will be okay, but in my Native American class, some here don't even know they are Native. I believe the school should allow Native teachers to come in and teach our language."

Grade 11. "What it means to be Ojibwe: I am typically seen as a White or mixed girl. I always find myself correcting people, that I am a role member of the Turtle Mountain Reservation. At school I play varsity sports and take challenging classes. Outside of school, I do pow-wow, and I do dance. I'm very proud to be who I am as an Ojibwe, yet no one knows. My only wish is to let people know how we do exist."

Many Native students became involved in furthering awareness in school, asking for a culture class, wanting more Native history to be taught. Many complained, "Why it is only on Indian *month* that others know we are Indian?"

One student stated that his school "should teach more about Native American heritage, so they can learn about how important it is, and how it all started. Instead of having only the Native American students learn about their heritage, that should be taught to the whole class."

Students often said they felt they still won't be heard, even though nowadays they have "the right" to speak their concerns. On the school calendar, students were asked to put in writing what they might want to do, but their requests seemed to fall on deaf ears. The number of American Indian students in these schools was small. Some Indian students were given the opportunity to learn Indian history, but only if their teacher was comfortable enough and willing to do justice to the topic.

In US history class, when they come to the chapter on Native Americans, some reported that little time is spent on the subject; the teacher goes over the chapter quickly. Individual Indian students are frequently compared to all Indians. Native students are often singled out during a history lesson, they are asked questions that suggest they represent or have to answer for all Native Americans. Being treated with such discrimination feels uncomfortable to young people. The education system tends to label native students in ways that set them up to fail or be shamed for not believing in themselves.

The best teachers are inventive with any disenfranchised student, providing resources instead of judgments so they can be successful.

Each school year, the situation was a bit different, but the education system basically failed Native American students and their families by not taking a more holistic teaching approach. Kids being judged by test scores causes many students to fail and be labeled in "special education" classes; and special education then failed (and still fails) to provide the services to meet the child's needs.

I have worked with young Indians whose parents felt they were not heard or listened to. Like any parents wanting their children to be successful, they want to work at the school and help to meet their child's needs. If their child has a learning disability, parents want to address it and understand the language of the testing process.

The school environment is uncomfortable and not welcoming for Native parents. Meeting with the school often feels threatening to Indian parents who feel the school is not listening to them. Many Indian parents have questions and concerns about how their child is being disciplined, wanting to understand fully why any discipline is used. Why are Indian students dismissed or suspended more than White students?

Native students often find it difficult to feel part of school. They feel overlooked. Many have said that nothing at school looks like them; they feeling invisible and not heard. Their identity as an Indian is questioned with remarks such as: "You're a Native American Indian? You don't look like an Indian."

Hidden prejudice is passed on nonverbally. Some White people will say out loud that the "past" treatment of Indian people was horrific, but the unspoken prejudice still continues.

I've heard it said that racism is "ignorance" on the part of the uneducated who don't know about, or want to know about, their own participation in it. Talking about the treatment of non-Whites throughout US history, they will often say, "That all that happened a long time ago. Get over it."

Yet we still hear the old stereotypes and find no true history books that describe Native peoples with respect. There is no acknowledgment of those who speak two languages—the Native language doesn't count. If a student speaks and understands a Native language, this should be honored and count as an added language for college entry.

America has so many nationalities and languages. People from other countries can speak their birth language freely, have their own place to worship. They're allowed to keep whatever they came with, including what they believe and their customs from their home country.

I can't help thinking that we should be more advanced and sophisticated by now in the twenty-first century. Public schools receive federal dollars for each student.

~

I felt honored when students shared some of their stories with me, stories within a broad spectrum of feelings from tears and sadness to how each had so much joy to give. Each had a uniqueness and quality of being themselves, they were smart and talented young people.

I had the opportunity to see each one mature. I watched how the young men's voices got squeaky and they some looked awkward for a time, and the young women giggled and tried to find just where they fit in. My biggest pleasure was working with them from middle school through high school, and now they are adults with children of their own, and part of a community.

Chapter 12

Returning to Marty

I drove by the Marty boarding school many times on the way to Native American Church ceremonies with my mother over the years. I figured if I kept going by, I would at some point have the nerve to deal with this anger and pain, and how the abuse affected my life. But I was still too attached to all of it.

Until I was in my thirties, I wasn't aware that my own mother had gone to Marty. It was when her family became homeless when she was only nine. She had never talked about it or brought it up before. That brief conversation only happened once as we were coming back from a ceremony in Greenwood, South Dakota.

Marty was like a ghost town by then, and we always passed the old boarding school on the way home from visiting relatives and attending NAC ceremonies. I said I wanted to stop and take some pictures now that the school was empty. The school name had been changed in 1975 to Marty Indian School and was now owned and operated by the Yankton Sioux Tribe.

We walked around the grounds a bit, but we could not go inside.

Here was where, for the first time, I asked my mother about us girls having to go to Marty. It wasn't a disrespectful way of asking her, but she remained quiet.

When I asked again, she sounded angry. She said, "Go look at the little house in the back. That was the first building."

Then she said something about "an orphanage." She said her mother dropped her off to stay and go to school there.

Surprised, I asked, "Did you like it?"

She said, "Yes."

She said it was warm and had food, and kids her age to play with.

That's all she would say.

~

In 2008 my husband suggested a trip to South Dakota during spring break from my job as a social worker with middle school and high school students. He thought it would be fun for our grandchildren and our son to see the Black Hills. I tried to be positive and see that idea as a good thing, but I really just wanted to stay home and get some rest.

Going to the Black Hills wasn't a big deal to me, and I hadn't forgotten the home where I was raised in South Dakota; but after living in Minnesota more than thirty years, I'd been gone for so long that most of the people I loved were gone. I missed the two people who were most important to me; Uncle and Auntie were no longer alive. Seeing them as my parents did a lot for me. They gave me love and encouragement, and I had always wanted to make them proud: my uncle, especially because he felt it was important to work in the Indian community. He told me that maybe that was what I supposed to do. "Go get an education and come back and work for people." Like a father to me, Uncle told me that it is okay to go somewhere else to do this work.

Back then I had prayed, asking the Creator, *If this is the right way, give me the courage to be strong.* Life took me in a different directions, but always toward helping young Native people.

I now considered Minnesota my home, my community. I'm happy in the Twin Cities, where it's large enough to go about your business. My Indian community is here. I'm happy and welcome. Even people from different tribes still have something in common: being Indian. For me, the great opportunity here in the Cities is to do work that helps the Indian community. Supporting professionals and nonprofessionals has been the biggest gift I had while working with my students. I could work and socialize in the Indian community. This is home, where different tribes all come together, not judging each other on where they are enrolled. This is a community I'm proud to be part of, and I hope that one day we will have one tribe and still honor each other's birthright.

The last time I had been in Pine Ridge was when I was in college. I have relatives buried at Wounded Knee, and some who still lived in Pine Ridge. Though Pine Ridge was where my father was an enrolled member, his decision not to go to Pine Ridge when we were very young meant that we never got to know our relatives on that reservation. My father, who is buried there with many other relatives, made this decision not to go back to live or to raise his family on *any* reservation—he knew it would be a hard struggle to feed his family.

I finally agreed to the trip to South Dakota when I figured we could also get some business done. Our son needed a tribal picture ID with his enrollment number on it to prove he's Indian to be eligible for funding for school, and my daughter and I needed updated tribal IDs. So the plan was to go directly to the Indian office, take a picture for a new ID, and be on our way. My daughter's two kids came with us. I also planned to visit a friend who moved from the Twin Cities back to Pine Ridge.

Pine Ridge had not changed very much. Some of the buildings were new, but I saw the despair and poverty. Indian country is the poorest in the US. Some call it the third world. No jobs, poor healthcare, the highest death rate among the youth. Anyone lucky enough to work would be in the schools, as teachers or support staff. Pine Ridge and Marty both had new schools. The teachers' pay was low; a rural reservation was unable to attract and keep good teachers.

The demeanor of the people we saw conveyed an unhappy feel. They had no interest in speaking to a stranger, even an Indian. The place had the strong scent of distrust. I knew this behavior, it felt familiar, like part of the Indian soul and community. In such a close-knit community, it takes time for them to speak to new strangers.

I felt good at least knowing this was where my father had once lived, and of course I wished the people I loved from my tiospaye were still living there. I missed the humor and safety; I claimed this for my Minnesota community. We are from different tribes, speak different Indian languages, but I feel part of the Indian community. We all care for one another, we want to see all our young Indians be successful, encourage them to be proud and feel that "this is my community." Standing in this place, I thought, *I'm comfortable, happy, and enjoy working for my community.*

We went to a powwow and visited my grandfather's grave at

Wounded Knee. It had changed. The little white church was no longer there. The graveyard was well kept with a memorial for all the ones who were "killed" in the massacre at Wounded Knee.

I remembered my grandfather holding an eagle feather as he sang and prayed and shared its powerful message at the end of the ceremony. "Wait, it will come to you, whatever your need may be, be respectful, and listen. Be humble, stand tall with your posture straight, never hang your head, we are very proud people."

Being on "my" reservation, I couldn't help but notice Marty school was right in front of me, along with all the bad memories. Though I had passed Marty many times over the years, I was going to do something I promised myself that I would never do again—this time I thought we could make a brief stop and look at the school. The Marty I knew was no longer in operation of course. The monies had dried up. I felt so happy that it closed, but it's such a waste that all the empty buildings can't be used for something positive. The tribe could run it if they chose to.

I had told my daughter a little bit about my time at Marty Indian Mission. She knew how painful and damaging the emotional abuse was for me. Even though it was still raw, I shared as much as I could with her. She always listened to me. I appreciated and could feel her support.

I did not want to stay long. I felt like that little Indian girl the day I was dropped off. In my mind she is the one I kept deep inside if I ever thought of those times and felt scared. I felt like I never grew up. Those feelings of anxiety, fear, loneliness, afraid I was going to get in trouble. I shared only enough, keeping it vague, to prevent me from getting depressed and angry.

My mother never answered much about how we ended up at Marty. She never questioned me either about my time there, not wanting questions. I told her what I felt comfortable telling her; the rest were hidden secrets. I never told her about the abuse. I had stuffed all that too deep.

I knew my daughter loved me. I trusted her. I didn't want her to hurt or feel my pain, only I would deal with this. She knew it was hard for me. She never once said anything; she just listened and held my arm. I felt her support and love. Never once did I hear her say "Get over it" or, "It never happened because I never talked about it, nor did my sisters."

My sisters and I stuffed the childhood trauma as we grew up to be adult women. When I think of those memories, my chest is heavy, it is hard to breathe, then everything comes racing back. It is hard to focus. I want to forget, to go on with my life. It wasn't possible, but it was part of me.

In taking a big step to begin a healing process, by walking through my childhood nightmare at Marty Indian Mission boarding school, I gained confidence by having my daughter with me. We walked arm in arm. No one was there; the grounds were quiet and creepy. It was instantly painful for me just be standing there, anxious, scared, and very sad. I saw my deepest feelings and secrets, being terrified, getting lost.

I will never be found. Will I ever get to go home?

But I really wanted to get over that feeling of being abandoned. I wanted that answer for my younger sisters as well. So I decided that I have to feel that I'm in control.

Okay, I decided, *I will face it, and if I back out, I will know that I'm not ready yet.*

I started to tell my daughter about all the rules we had to obey. How if we broke any, we were punished severely.

The church was gone, and our tribal office was housed in the old nunnery. The place felt taboo to me, off limits. I had a feeling that I was about to be yelled at, scolded, punished. The buildings were old and had weathered over time, but the structure outside looked the same. The grounds were well kept; it looked like a college campus, if you didn't know better.

We went to the rectory where the priest used to live. Now only three of the nuns stayed back to take care of the church and teach catechism. I did not remember ever meeting the nun we talked to, Sister M. She remembered one of my sisters, and she remembered me.

I asked her if I could go into the buildings, she said she didn't have the keys. We'd have to go to the tribal office and get permission from the superintendent. She said the building was unstable, the foundation was bad. But it looked the same. She offered to show me the church.

No longer was there holy water in the entry. As I walked in, it was quiet, but it still had an echo. All the little confessionals were gone. I felt strange not having to cover my head or kneel before sitting down in a pew. I never really understood why we had to cover our heads or put our fingers in the holy water and make a cross. I just did what I had to do.

I didn't feel comfortable being there. It was taboo, like regressing back to those days. Over the years, I got so comfortable not thinking about it.

Yet this little girl inside me was saying, *No! Speak up and tell them what happened was not okay. You won't be harmed now.*

I never honored that little girl when she was hurting badly. I just swallowed that lump in my throat and cleared my voice. I never thought I was worth it. I wondered if anyone knew or cared. Back then, I just thought, *Please come and take me away from this place. I promise I will never say or bring up Marty.*

The nun asked how we were doing. I told her what I'd been doing and what kind of career I had, that I now had the family I wanted when I was little.

She told me, "Ah, you had the opportunity to see the outside world after leaving Marty."

I asked about the girl who bullied me. The nun said she still lives on the reservation and hasn't gone anywhere. She took care of her grandchildren.

We continued walking around the campus and visited the places I was not allowed to go before. I visited the old school. No longer a mission school. Now they had high school boarders, twenty students who volunteered to live and go to a new high school that was built after the old boarding school closed.

Physically being at Marty, looking back, I felt the separation, the loss of being with my friends and my little sisters. For years, this place had never existed, it still felt dark with no good memories. The forgotten little Indian child, who I carried inside, took on the responsibility, carried this burden. Now her true smile was hidden deep inside along with her secrets.

I thought of myself and my four little sisters, "the Marty five." We were so young, feeling like five little birds that fell out of the nest, not ready to fly, left alone, and helpless. I was still full of anger, I couldn't forgive those involved. Even though I was educated and had a good life and loving family, regardless of what anyone says, the pain still laid heavy in my heart.

If only I could go back to comfort that little Indian girl in those dark days. If I could go back to that time, I would take this little brown Indian girl in my arms and tell her it's going to be okay, and no one will hurt you or treat you mean or nasty.

I would hold her hand, and we would talk to all those grownups and tell them, "This is wrong, and this has to stop, or you will get into a lot of trouble."

After that, we would continue on to all those dark places that scared her so much. I will hold her hand tight to let her know I won't let go, that I am there to protect her and not harm her. If you call out my name, you can be sure I will be there for you. You will never hear me say, "Wait." I will always be with you, don't worry. You can be honest. You don't have to fake your true feelings in order to get my attention; my love is not pretend or fake.

In my mind I pictured this golden-brown Indian girl in a little green dress with a trace of red around her collar and green trim in fringe around her waist, and long, black braided hair, as she stepped into our childhood nightmare. I was going to help this little Indian girl who stuffed so many losses for so long.

I will accept her, appreciate her with her golden-brown, perfect round lips that seldom ever had a real smile. She never got a chance to grow up to live fully without the embarrassment and shame I feel. She also wanted to forgive herself, knowing it wasn't her fault, not doing or saying anything to them. It was *their* fault.

My little Indian girl lived within this pain and never felt safe for a long time.

This was the first time I acknowledged the pain of this little girl who had been frozen in the past. My emotion was raw, remembering all the harsh punishment, being disciplined by a stranger at an institution of people who worshiped Jesus, God.

I told myself that I will nurture myself now, tell myself that I'm okay. I have the power to let her know I am in control. I wanted to be here with the little girl, we would unite together in facing what I didn't want to know about how we were profoundly affected by the experiences at Marty.

I looked in her eyes and asked, *Why do you frown when you look like you're going to cry? I love your beautiful golden-brown skin. I love you no matter what. You're laughing that bright smile. This time I will be the adult keeping you near me. I will shelter you from the ones who want to hurt us again. Knowing you were hurting inside for such a long time, feeling you couldn't talk about this emotion, it is time to open up about that and I will not leave you behind.*

For all those years, I had to find the tools within, without feeling foolish, knowing that others hadn't found the answers either to the questions we sought to heal. I wondered how many of the boarding school students had ever returned to Marty.

Looking at all the empty dorms and other buildings, I felt the presence of the Catholic Church again, the nuns, brothers, and fathers, and I suddenly felt scared. I regressed to feeling like a child again. The creepy feelings began all over again.

So why in hell did I put myself through this once again?

I wanted and needed to find my voice, mostly gain power over being shamed, hurt, abused, bullied. I had cursed that bully over and over, and it took a great deal of energy to stay angry all these years; the effects of being bullied affected my entire life. And in all that time, I never had a chance to find that little golden-brown girl who was forced to stay quiet. *Who would believe her anyway?* I looked like an adult, yet I still hurt deep inside along with her secrets.

I knew it would be hard to do this.

The golden-brown Indian girl was anxious, looking around.

How can I make this little girl I carried deep inside not be afraid?

In my mind, I held her little hand; it was trembling, my heart was hurting.

I told her, "No one will harm you or punish you. No nun will hit you or tell you that you are uncivilized, no good, or not loved." I reassured her she will not be staying; we are going home together.

I glanced at the empty field of the playground where only one lonely swing was left after all those years. It looked like the same old swing I used to sit.

I thought I would never want to have to deal with all this now, or ever. I'm no longer child or have to be at boarding school. I can protect myself now if another bully enters my life. I stay away from toxic people. I learned was to see how foolish people can be and to "trust my gut."

I learned young to be careful, be alert, guard my space. Bullies never stop, they only grow up. They all come in all shapes. I had learned not to give 100 percent in relationships, just give enough, never reveal what can be used against you. Guard what you have that is sacred. Dignity and self-worth are something to hold onto. I told myself that nothing lasts forever. I do exist. I believe in my Creator.

My eyes are open now, seeing the truth of what Marty Mission School stood for. Just like the now-empty buildings, the truth is no longer hidden. I know Marty carries my history just as that of many other students who were emotionally wounded there. The buildings are still standing, I'm still standing. But it has been painful for me.

Many years after leaving the school, I sometimes felt I was getting good at turning off the abusive tape recorder in my head. I repeated, *You're okay, slow down*, if something triggered that feeling of going back to being that scared little girl. I didn't want to hurt. Years of taking tiny steps, trying to forgive myself, stop the blaming. I couldn't stop remembering the past; it was bunched up all into one feeling. It was hard to explain. The school was closed; it could no longer hurt anyone, it was all in the past. My life had new stressful events, just like everyone else has in life. I had to stop those things that triggered the memories of feelings, words, anger, and stop living in the past. I didn't talk about my feelings of shame, guilt. I was embarrassed to let anyone know, not wanting to appear weak. Yet the horror revisited me. The effects of abuse are guaranteed to follow for the rest of adult life unless they are dealt with.

Now standing there on the school grounds in the presence of that little golden-brown Indian girl from long ago, and remembering the tears falling down our golden-brown face, I wanted to connect with her and put the pain away. I had to reassure myself and my inner child:

Nothing lasts forever. Unsolved deep sadness can't be our best friend. Stop these feelings of being enslaved in our past! Don't be swallowed by the past. Stay in the present. I'm in control. This time you will not be left alone. Most of all, you're not staying here, you are no longer, and will never be, made to stay at Marty Mission again. You are where you belong, you're with me, you are the treasure of me, our heart beats as one. You're safe now, you will never be abandoned. I am here. I love you.

Stand tall,
be proud,
you matter,
be brave, golden-brown Indian girl.

~

My journey was not yet completely over or healed from the boarding school. After that visit to Marty, I did a lot of soul searching, dealing more with the pain of boarding school. It was not easy to explain away what happened. I felt helpless, most of all powerless to do much of anything, because I believed all the lies the nuns told me—that I didn't matter. I was just a little Indian girl; if I disappeared, no one would miss me. In the White man's eyes I would be one less Indian taking up space. I internalized this cruelty.

I was not taught how to grieve or given the tools to. It had taken me a long time to find my way, to even know that something was wrong. Something was missing. I really didn't know why I always had this empty space in my heart, not feeling whole. I didn't know the past had anything to do with it.

I shared many deep secrets with my husband. He is a person who will listen and won't judge me or hold anything I say against me, or use it as a weapon to hurt me.

I took small steps.

I often told my husband that what I had gone through was like a scar in time; the mark would fade, get lighter. But the emotion is permanent and can come back in a minute. I hoped it would fade if I could work through all the feelings and stop shutting down.

I wanted to heal, stop hurting, stop blaming myself, stop feeling like a failure.

One evening after such a conversation, my husband said, "Let's go."

"What do you mean? Marty?"

"Yes, let's go to Marty."

I was surprised, "Really?"

He was willing to walk the grounds, go inside the buildings with me. He knew it was important for me to give it a try. For the first time since the school closed, I had a chance to be there with someone I trust who knew the deepest secrets.

I had to write a letter to the Bureau of Indian Affairs, asking the current BIA superintendent for permission to visit Marty. I called, and he said I could stop in the office to have someone let me into St. Theresa.

My husband and I got to Marty on a Friday. The tribal office had closed early and wouldn't be open until Monday. I sure didn't want to cut things short for us, and I didn't want to stay overnight. One good thing about the Yankton Reservation being so small was that we could ask around and find somebody who knew somebody who knew somebody. We got the permission we needed.

I was anxious and nervous. I didn't know how I was going to react this time. I felt like a little kid who was getting trouble. I was happy to have my husband with me. I wanted someone to witness this place for real, to come inside and see and touch the walls, stand on the floors. It excited me, wanting someone else who wasn't part of the Catholic Church to validate the experience that had impacted me in so many ways in my growing up. I was emotional, thinking, *Finally I will be listened to, and believed.*

My husband and I were about to visit and walk the grounds of Marty Indian Mission Boarding School together, and I knew this would be a painful step to take. I felt nervous, still carrying a lot of baggage with me. But I wanted to see it all as an adult who no longer felt helpless and powerless. With my husband there to witness each place I and my sisters has lived, I felt validated. I felt sad that the little Indian girl was not given a chance to have that type of support to heal and leave the pain behind on the day I walked away from Marty.

Because I wasn't ever allowed to visit my sisters, the little girls dorm on the third floor was the first place my husband and I went. The space was dim, quiet, no laughing of little girls. Seeing the double doors that had separated me from my little sisters, I felt lonesome again entering the big girls dorm through the same double door. Some of the windows in the dorm were broken from the outside. All the windows had curtains. I wondered if they were the same curtains.

Seeing the big room where our single metal beds had all been lined up, perfectly made, and the dorm nun's small room, a scary dark place, I felt all kinds of anxiety, fear, and jumpiness. Everything was gone, left to the elements, not kept up. The building was just like the other buildings, becoming unsafe.

The view through the third-floor window looked the same all those years later, and brought back memories of loneliness. There used to be more swings across from the girls dorms. Thinking back, how dark it was, the shadow of the building outside was pitch black, it was deep in the county. It reminded me of those scary movies about exorcism and evil. Those types of movies always happen in a Catholic Church, the priest in all black, carrying a cross.

On the second floor, we walked into my old classroom. First I remembered how it looked, all the desks lined neatly in perfect rows. I remembered looking out the window, daydreaming of being somewhere else, a happy place where I could look forward to talking to my friends. But now the room was empty, the window was broken; the curtain was torn and old. Some ceiling tiles were missing.

I remembered the time a nun got her habit caught in the closing classroom door, and her habit was almost pulled off. The whole class started to laugh. We all thought nuns were bald, all their hair cut off. We heard stories but didn't really know if they were true.

Because we students had strict boundaries; I never know what most of the buildings looked like inside. The superintendent office was where the nuns had lived. I asked if I could look around. He gave me permission to walk the floors that were not made into offices.

I looked in the empty rooms, thinking to myself that these are where the nuns slept, ate, and went to mass in the chapel. I have to admit, it was still frightening to feel like I might get caught, be grabbed by my hair, and told I had no business being in this area. The space didn't feel welcoming or friendly at all. I felt the same heavy feeling I always had about this place.

We walked the whole campus and went to all the places I wasn't allowed to go in the past. And the old tape recording in my mind kept playing, "I'm going to be punished or yelled at."

By the time we were done, I felt, *I'm in control now; I am not that little golden-brown Indian girl no one cared about or loved. I am all grown up and have come a long way. I had the courage to go.*

My only unfulfilled wish was that I could have spoken to two bullies, the dorm nun and the girl. I wanted to know why. I did learn that the nun, Sister B, was no longer a nun; she left. And the girl, she passed away. I don't feel hate for them or have regrets for not seeing them. Maybe this is how the Creator is showing me that this is a way of healing—by openly saying out loud that I suffered from abuse and emotional anguish that I carried silently throughout my adult life, never speaking about or sharing it with anyone, and letting shame and fear define me for a lifetime. I was finally going to put an end to my childhood nightmare. I didn't want to judge anyone I grew up with the way I was judged—with hate, jealousy. No more "What if?" or "If only. . ."

Funny how things turn out. Maybe this was what my uncle and auntie wished when they wanted me to help other Indian people. I laugh now because my life's work has always been in an educational setting, and that turned out to the biggest help for me. I could continue to be a support to Native young people, give students the tools to deal with and change what they can, and not see themselves in a negative way. I told them how what bullies say can hurt or offend a person, and destroy self-esteem.

I stayed strong and stubborn in believing what I was taught by my community and relatives who taught me the ways to pray, to be grateful for all the gifts, never be wasteful, that everything has a purpose, and never take or use more than you need. Give thanks and remember relatives who go on to the spirit world.

I cannot pretend that it is all better now for me. It comes and goes. I don't have any strong feelings left on my bad days or when something that reminds me how lonely I was back then. I'm working on my grief because I can't get back what had happened as a child.

The outside world is my community now. I have adjusted to a world society that doesn't say out loud that I don't belong here. Many of my relatives have their own lives. I have many friends and the support I need. I am still in contact with my first cousins; I am very close to them because my uncle and auntie let me live with them and gave me all the support, love, respect, and encouragement that basically saved my life.

All grown up, yet I still feel I should hide all the bad things that happened to me at Marty. To get to this point took me this long: becoming an elder; having my children grown up; having many losses; losing my oldest son, which broke my heart; then losing my older sister who was the matriarch of the seven of us sisters. She was a beautiful older sister, I had fun with her, we did things our mother will never know. Then my mother passed away a year after my older sister. However, though I wasn't always so good in following my own advice, I made sure I wouldn't become like those kinds of people without face who don't keep their promises. I have kept my promises to the little golden-brown girl. She is safe with me, and she knows she is loved.

Acknowledgments

First, my thanks to my Creator, Wakan Tanka, for all blessings.

I thank my awesome husband Leonard for reading an early draft of this book and giving me his advice. He always listened without judgment. I am thankful mostly for his believing me and for his personal support when we visited Marty and walked the boarding school grounds. He gave me empathy and hugs, he encouraged me to talk and not to be afraid to tell what really happened to me there, and he assured me that it would help with the healing. Throughout our marriage, he has been with me during my hardest times and losses. I also acknowledge with deep love my precious firstborn son, who died tragically and far too young.

I am grateful for my children, Tamika and Myles, who are both awesome, generous, loving humans, who are proactive in caring about human rights. I am thankful that they gave me the time to feel and talk about my experiences. Each has traveled with me many times on this difficult journey. My daughter is a caring soul with great empathy for others; my son, wanting to be my protector and feeling angry, always wanted to do something to make things right.

I honor my four younger sisters, who with me, I nicknamed the Marty five. They went through the same emotional impact, trauma, and hardships as I did. I give my respect to them. They grew up to be beautiful Dakota/Lakota Indian women. I only regret that two of my younger sisters went on to the spirit world, and their stories about the same hurt will not be told. My other two younger sisters have their own lives; both are strong and survived the hardships, though they don't talk openly about their experiences at Marty. One sister said, "Out of sight, out of mind."

I have the greatness love and respect for all my sisters.

I thank my coworkers who have listened and encouraged me to write this book. I'm glad to have them has my community; they have supported me in many ways. Thank you.

Thank you to my mentor, Kari Slade, who has been a teacher and become a great friend. She is a caring person who believes history should be told, and who gave me the courage to finish the book. I am so grateful that the Creator, Wakan Tanka, put people like her in my life, who have been contributors and advisors from the beginning to the end.

I couldn't have this book without my editor Marly Cornell. She is also an author with a passion for social justice. She took this book under her wing, helping me from the very beginning. I appreciate her guidance and caring to help finish my book in all the right ways. I couldn't ask for better than that.

About the Author

Artist, writer, and educator, Donna Council, was born on the Yankton Indian Reservation in South Dakota. Her family moved off the reservation to Mitchell, South Dakota, where she and her seven sisters began public school. She and four of her younger sisters were taken from their home and family by the BIA and enrolled in a government-mandated mission boarding school run by the Catholic Church on the Yankton Reservation, where she experienced the traumas described in this book. Donna went on to attend Presentation College in Aberdeen, SD, and earned a graduate degree in social work from Dakota Wesleyan. Over a forty-plus year career she served as a youth and family counselor, a guidance counselor, parent educator, and a culture coordinator in the public schools in Minneapolis and St Paul, Minnesota. She currently devotes her time to art and activism on behalf of disenfranchised Native youth.

Made in USA - North Chelmsford, MA
1363880_9798985639001
03.17.2023 0830